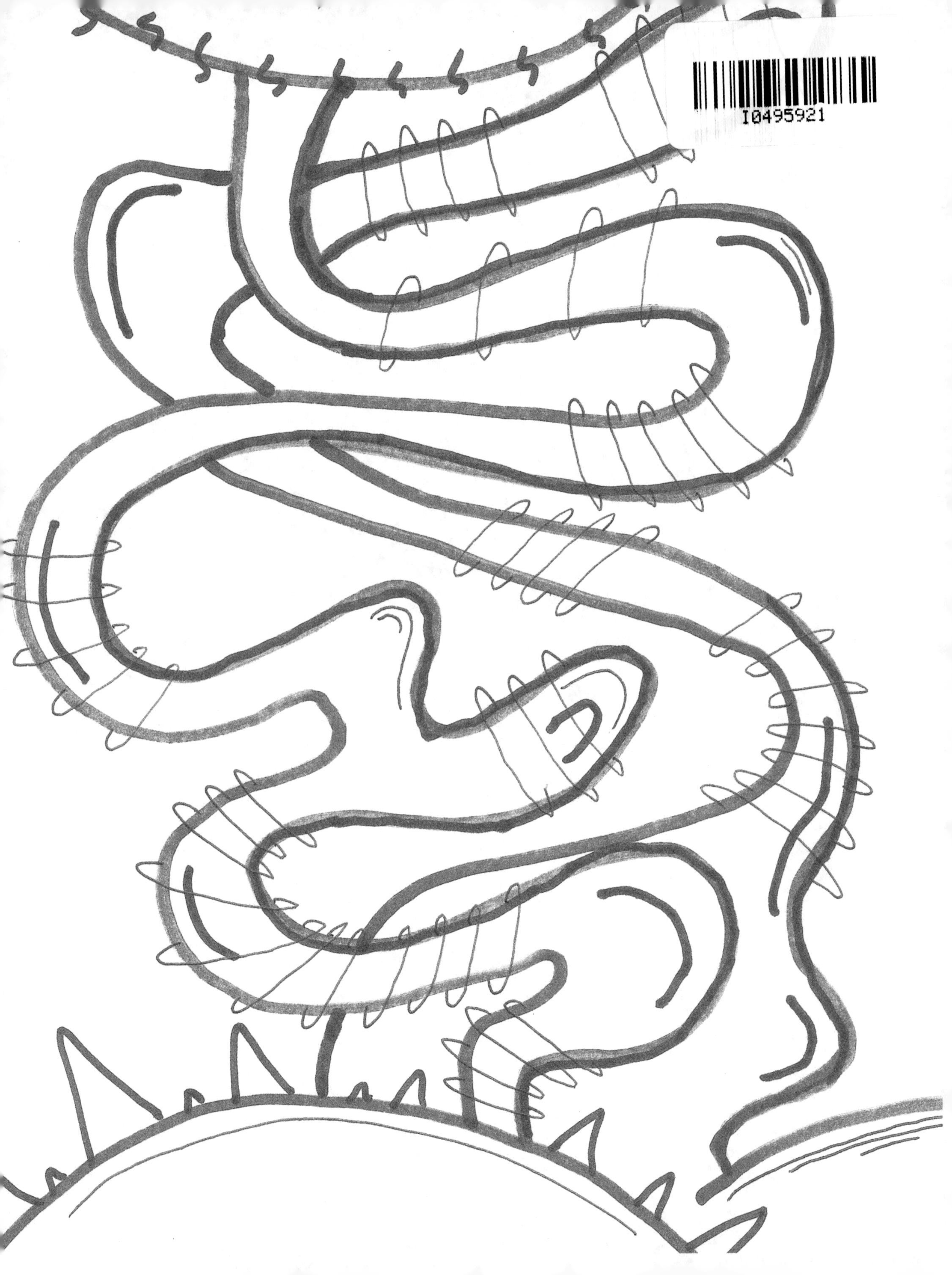

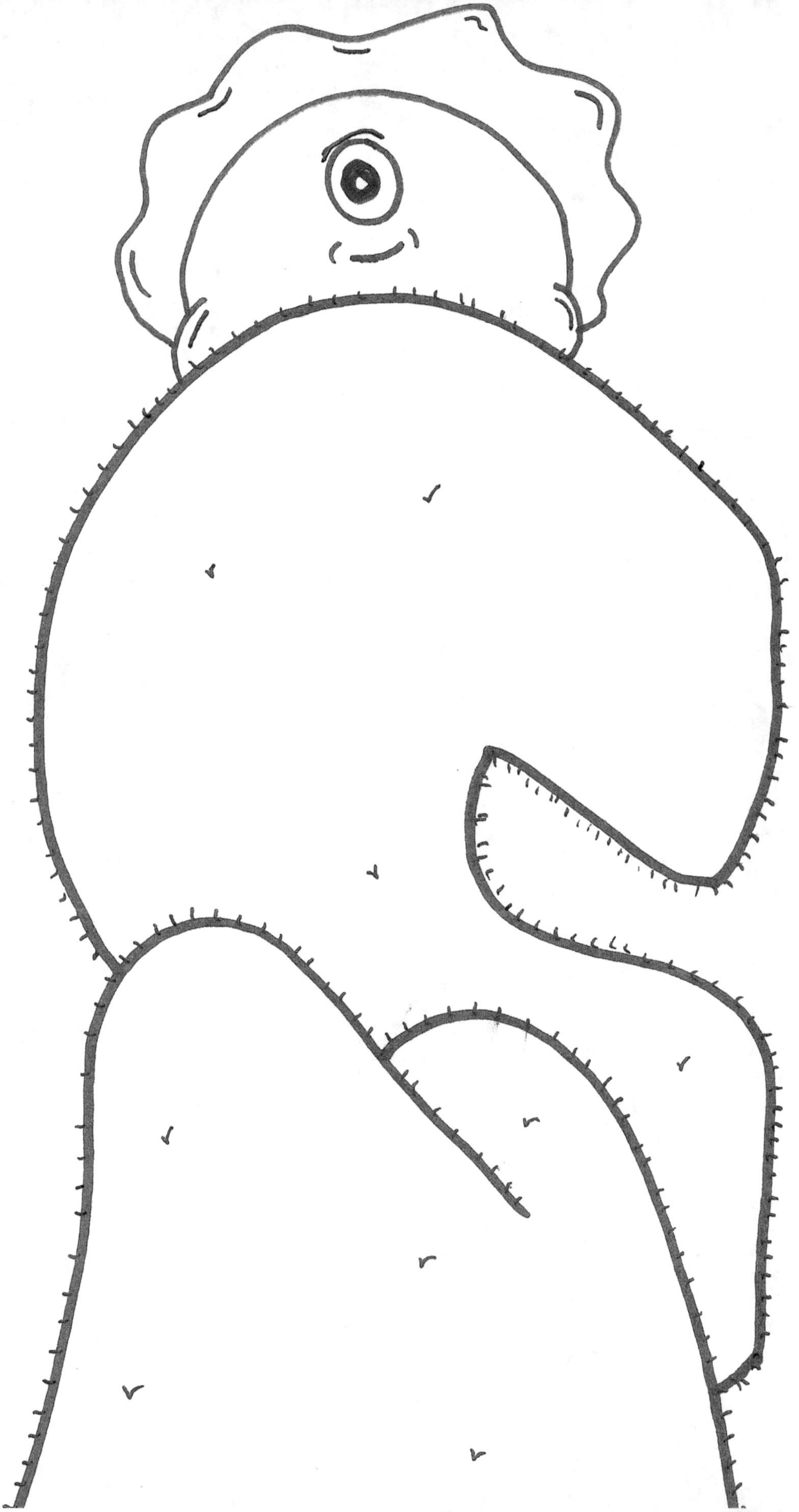

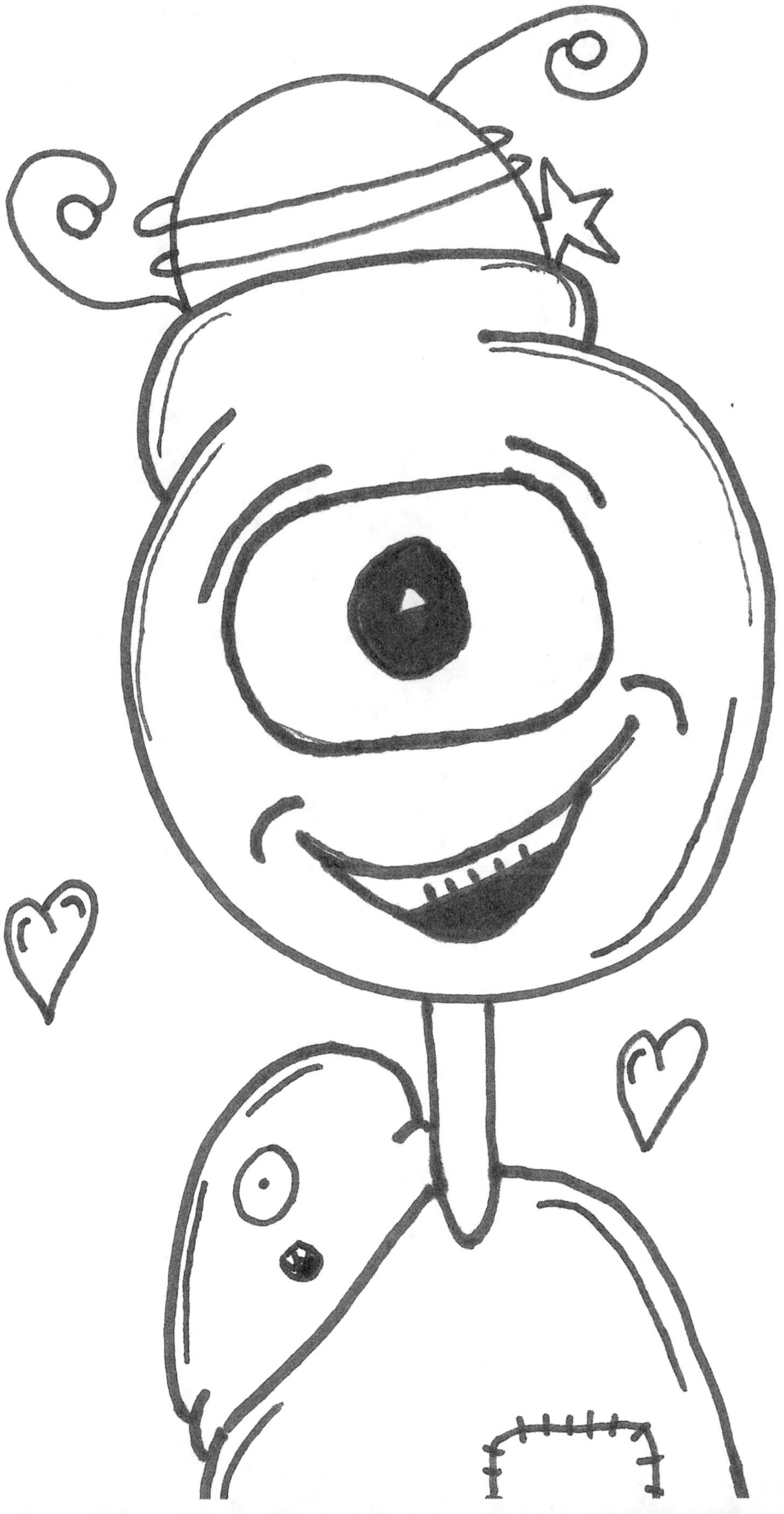

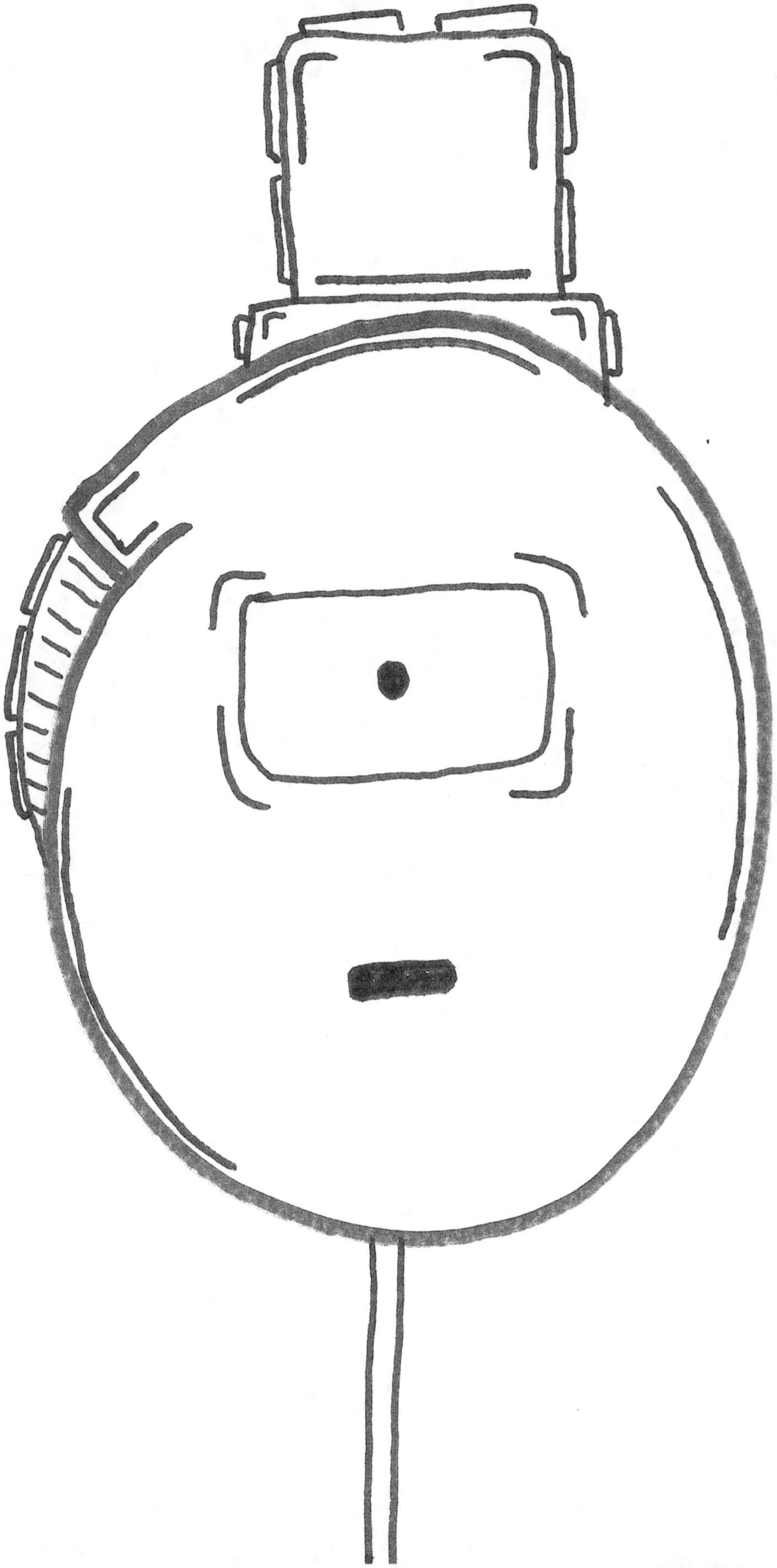

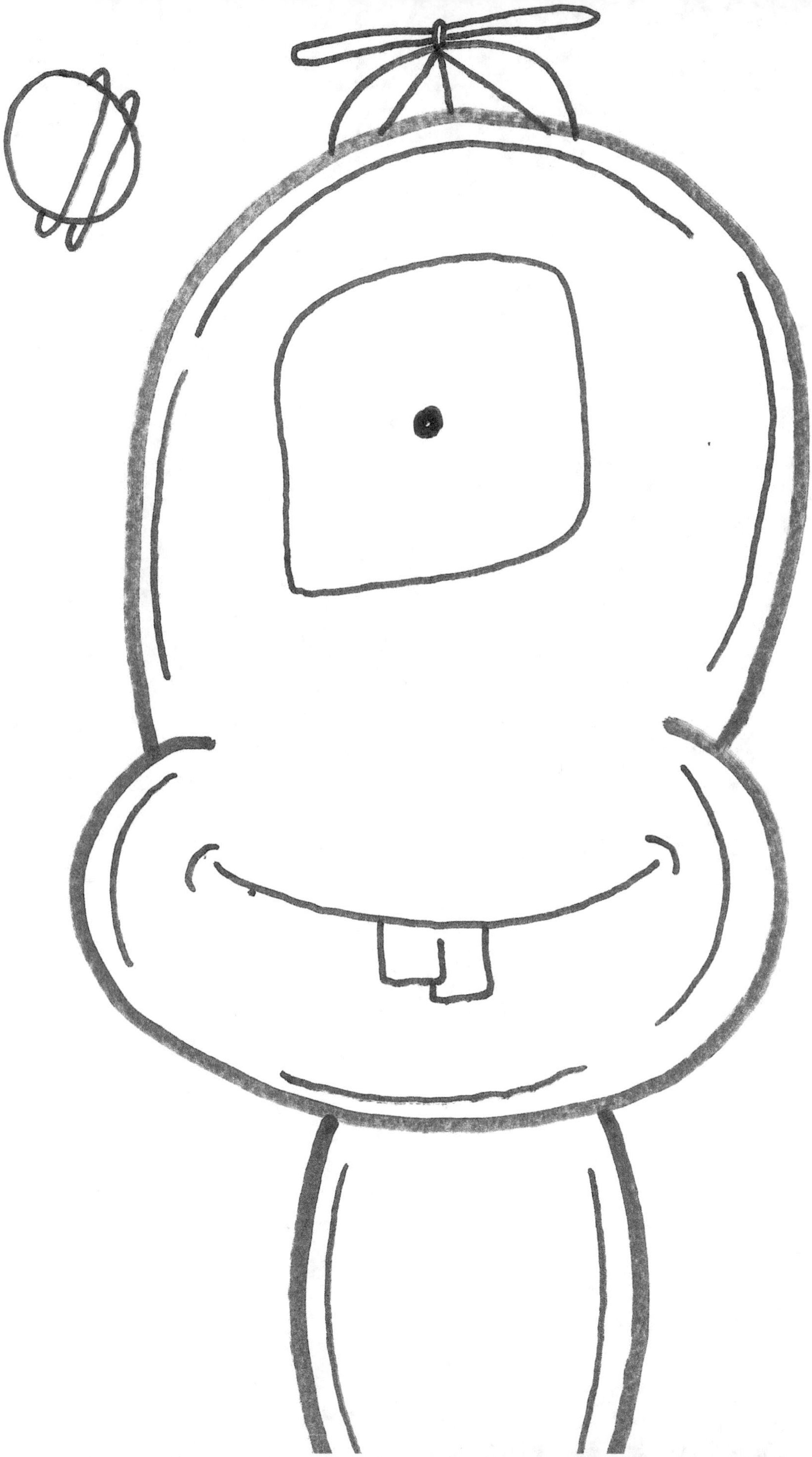

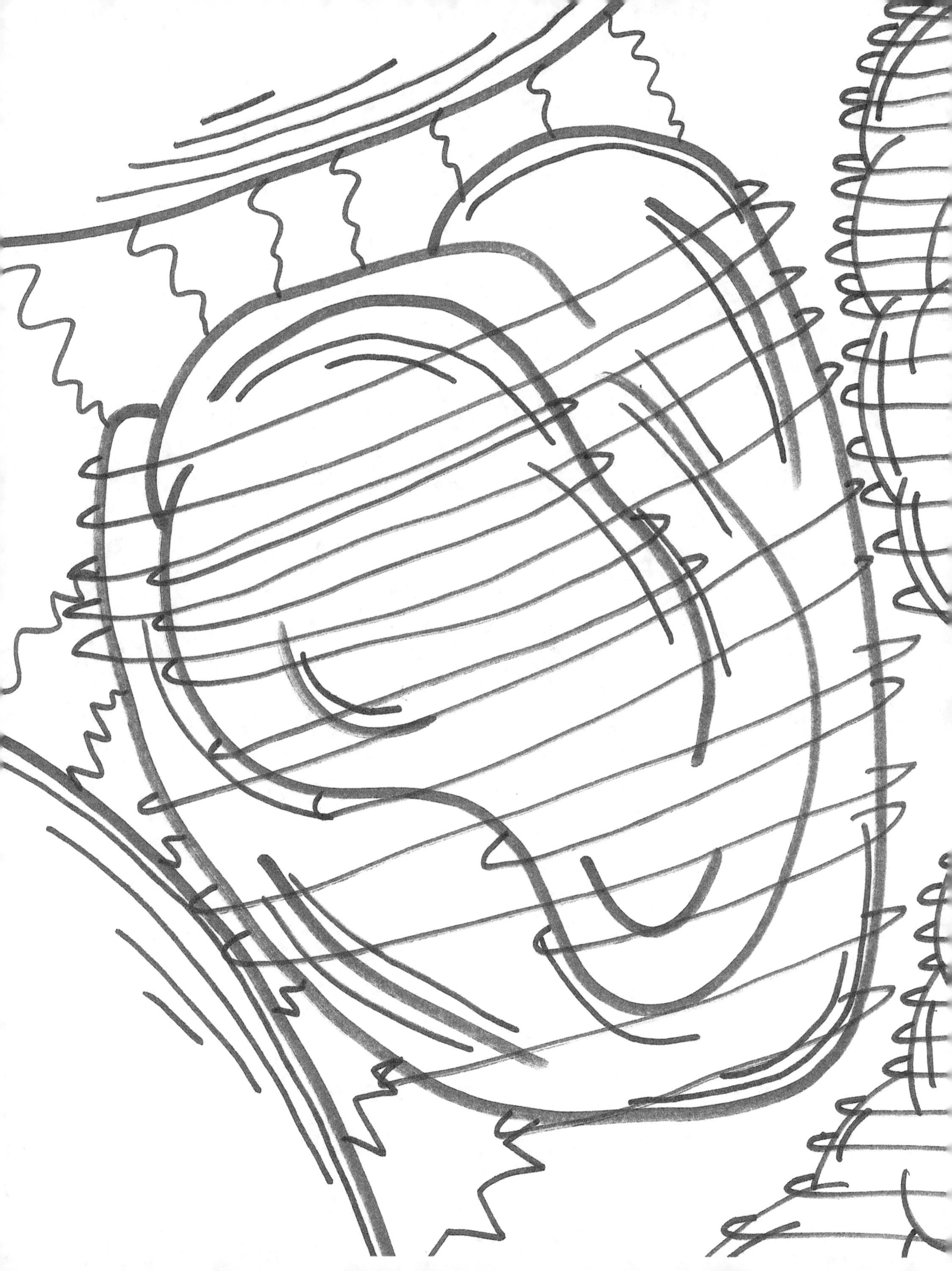

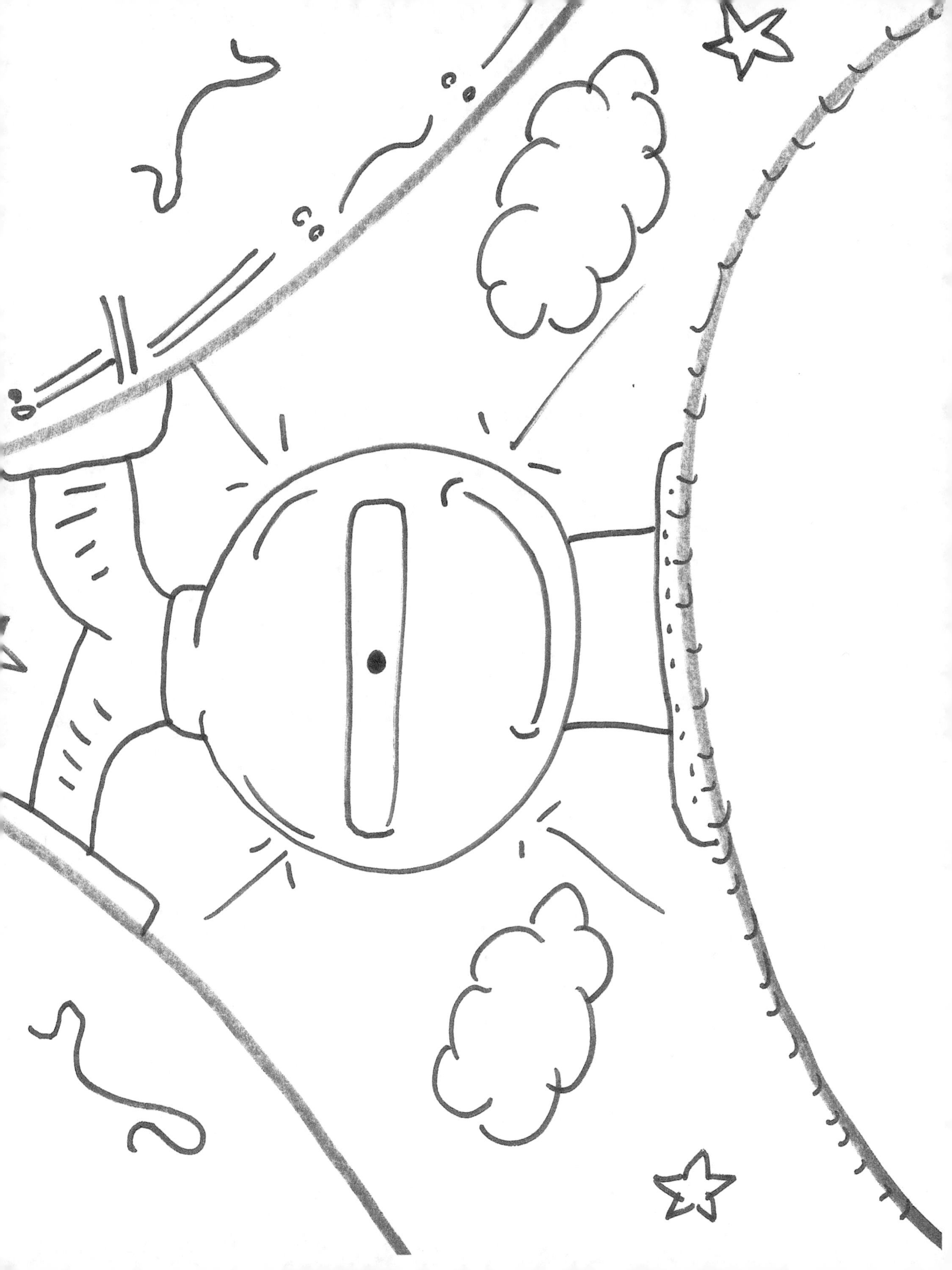

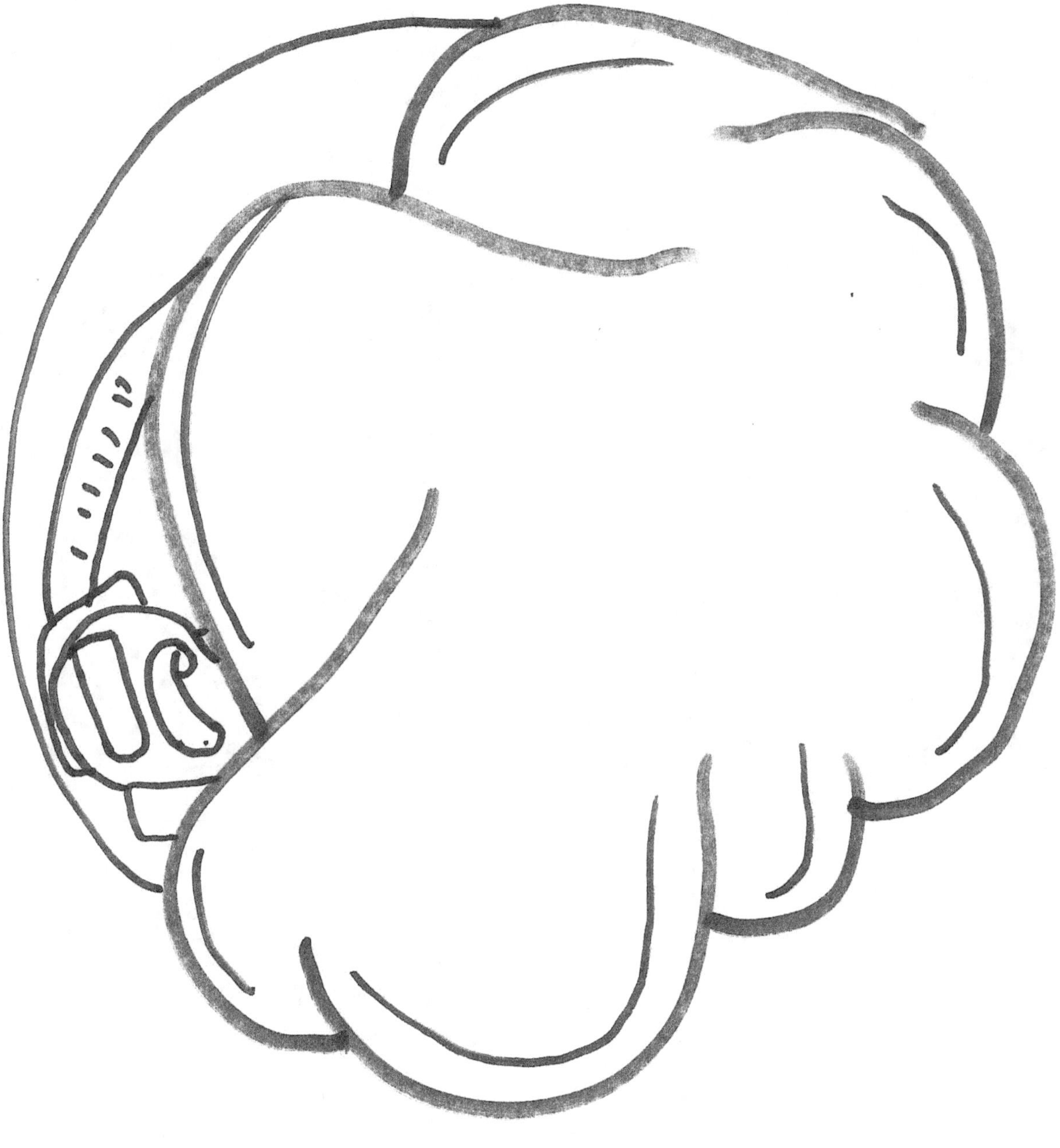

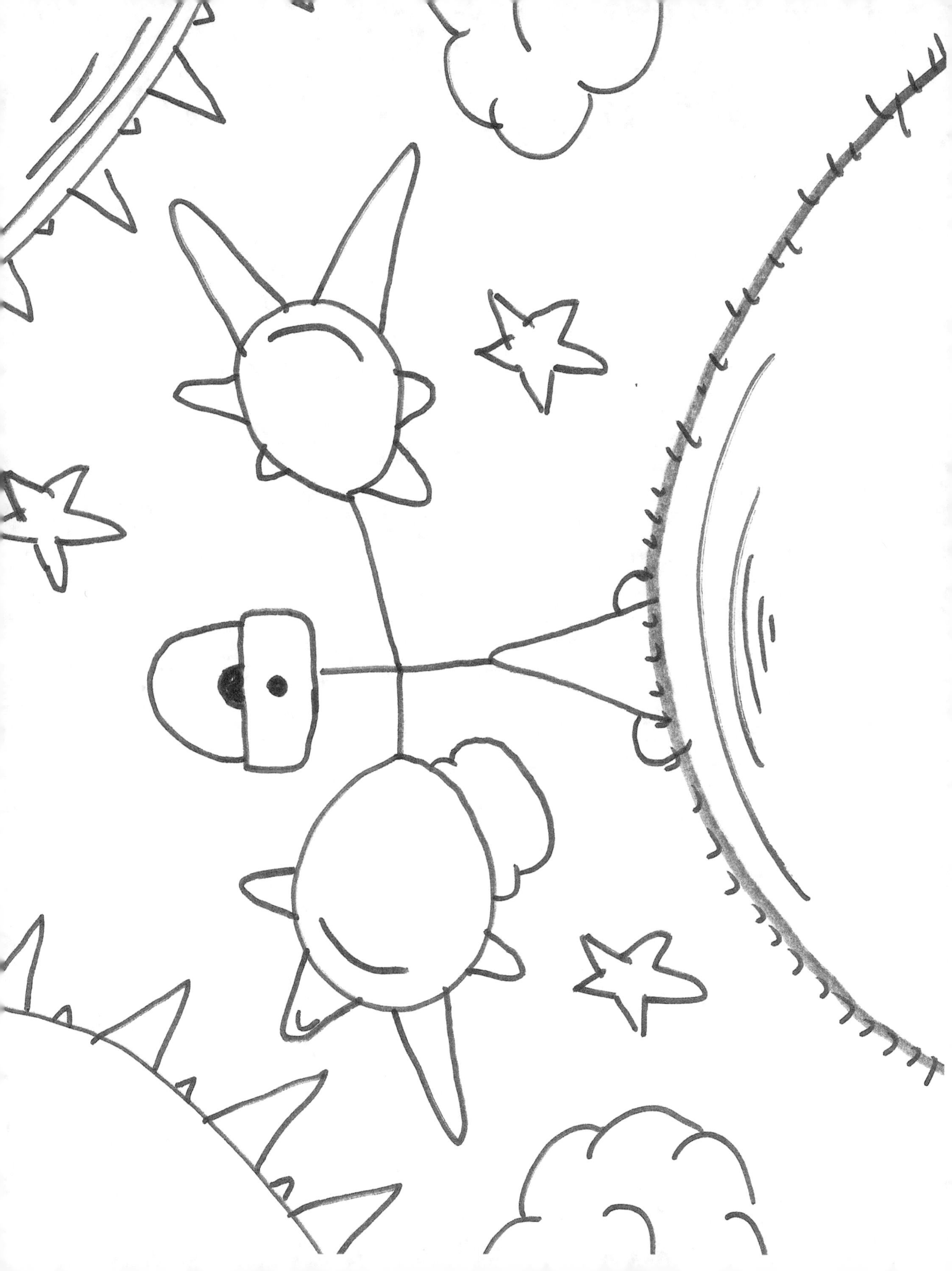

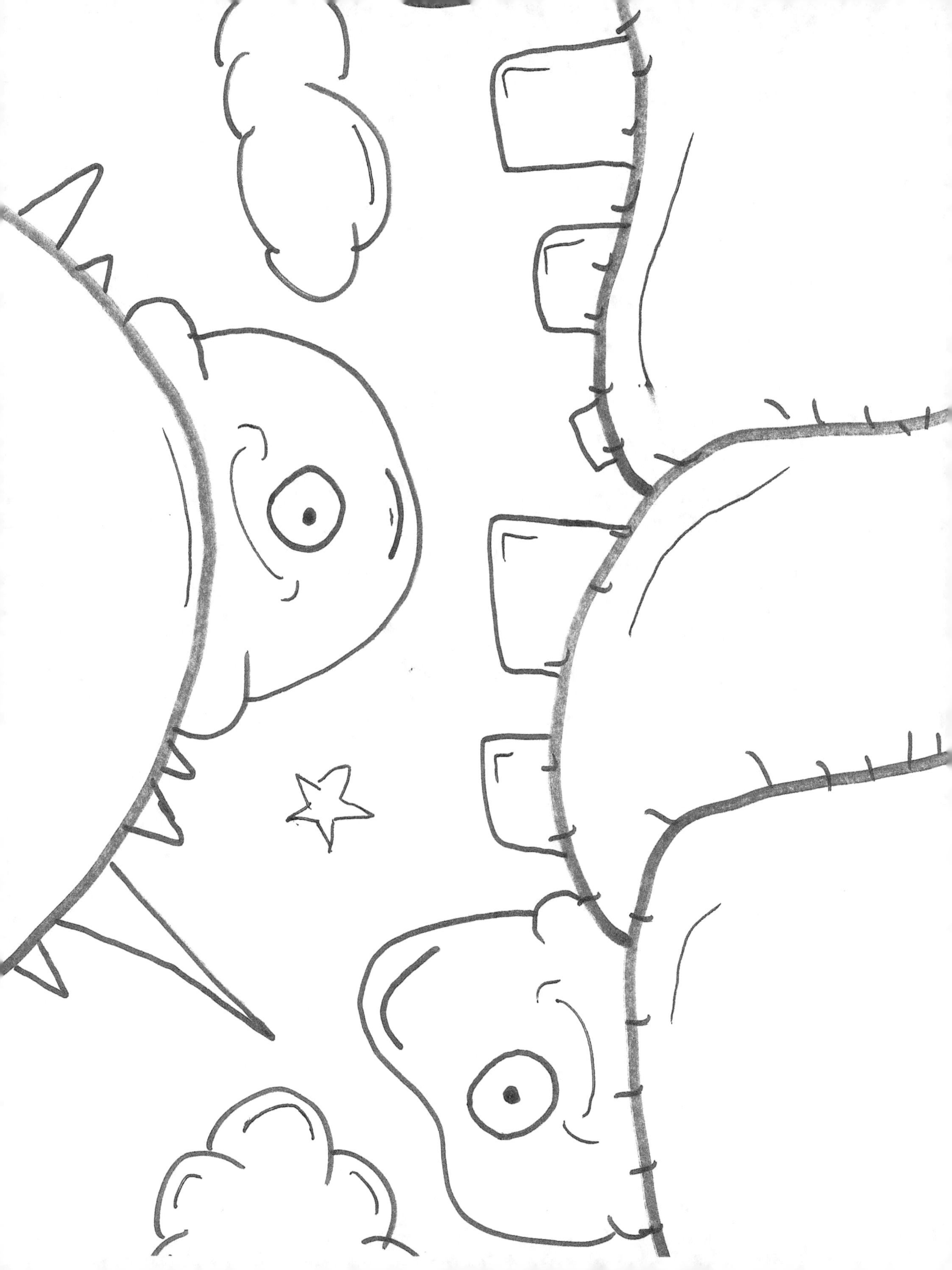

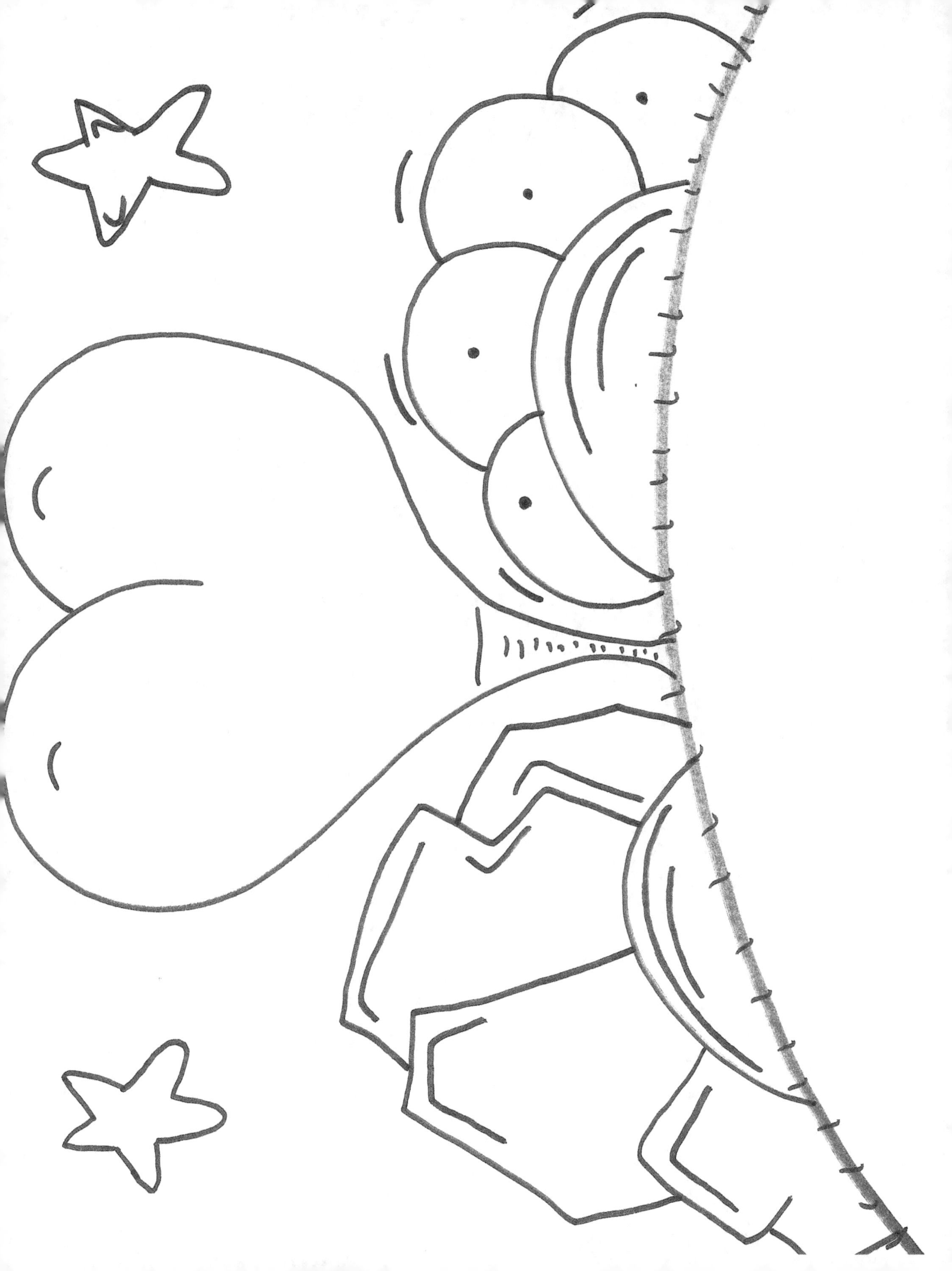

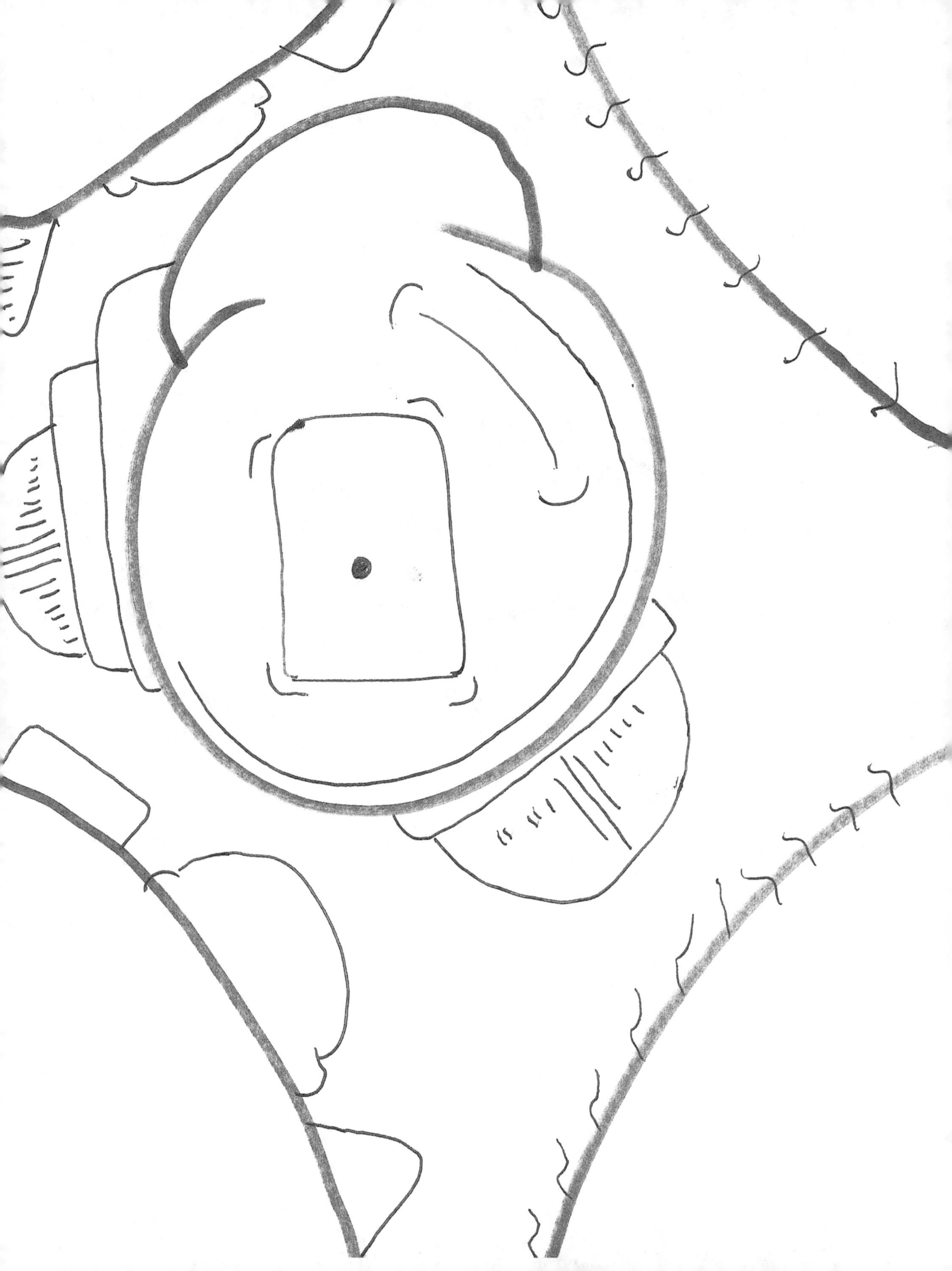

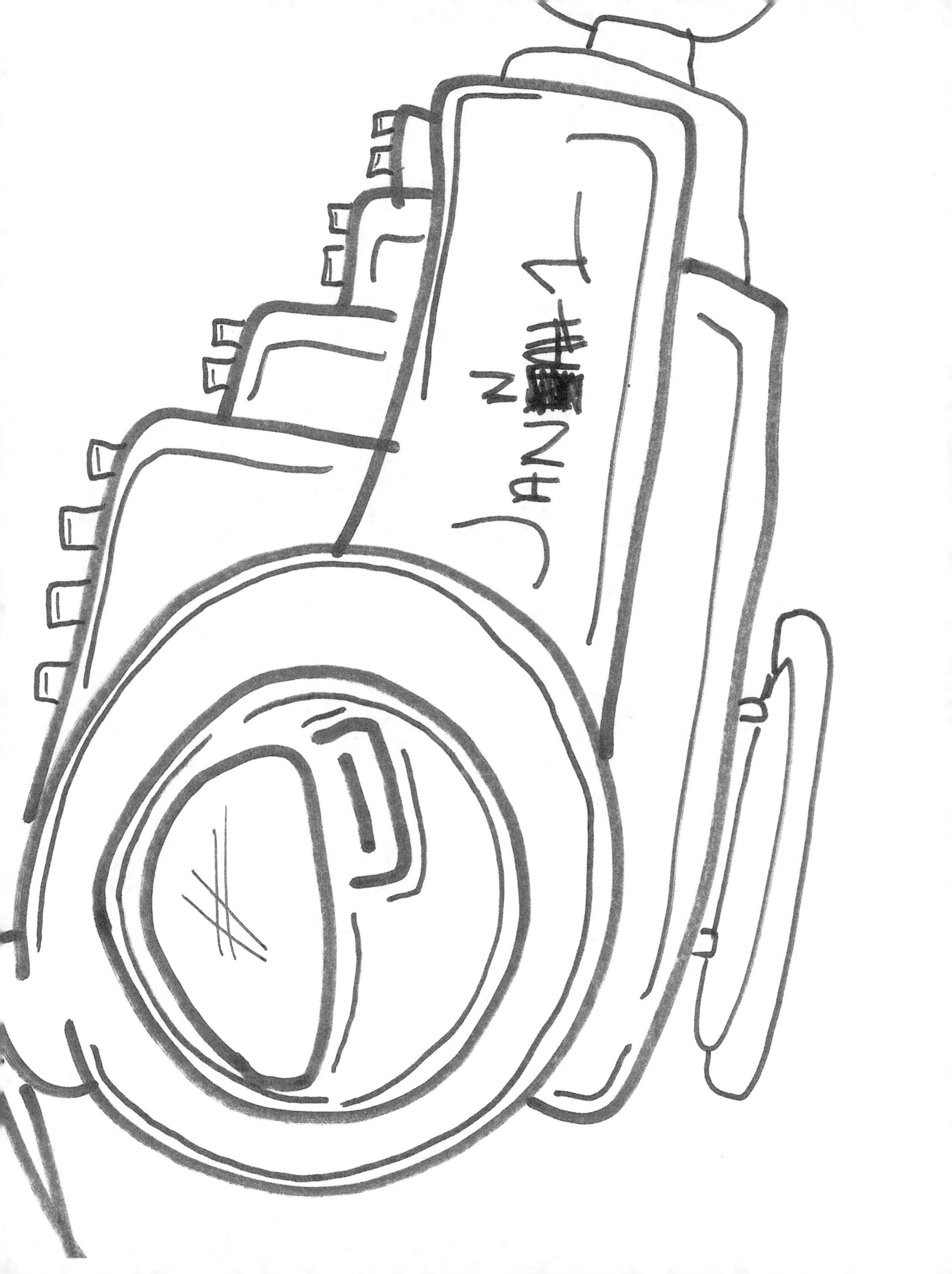

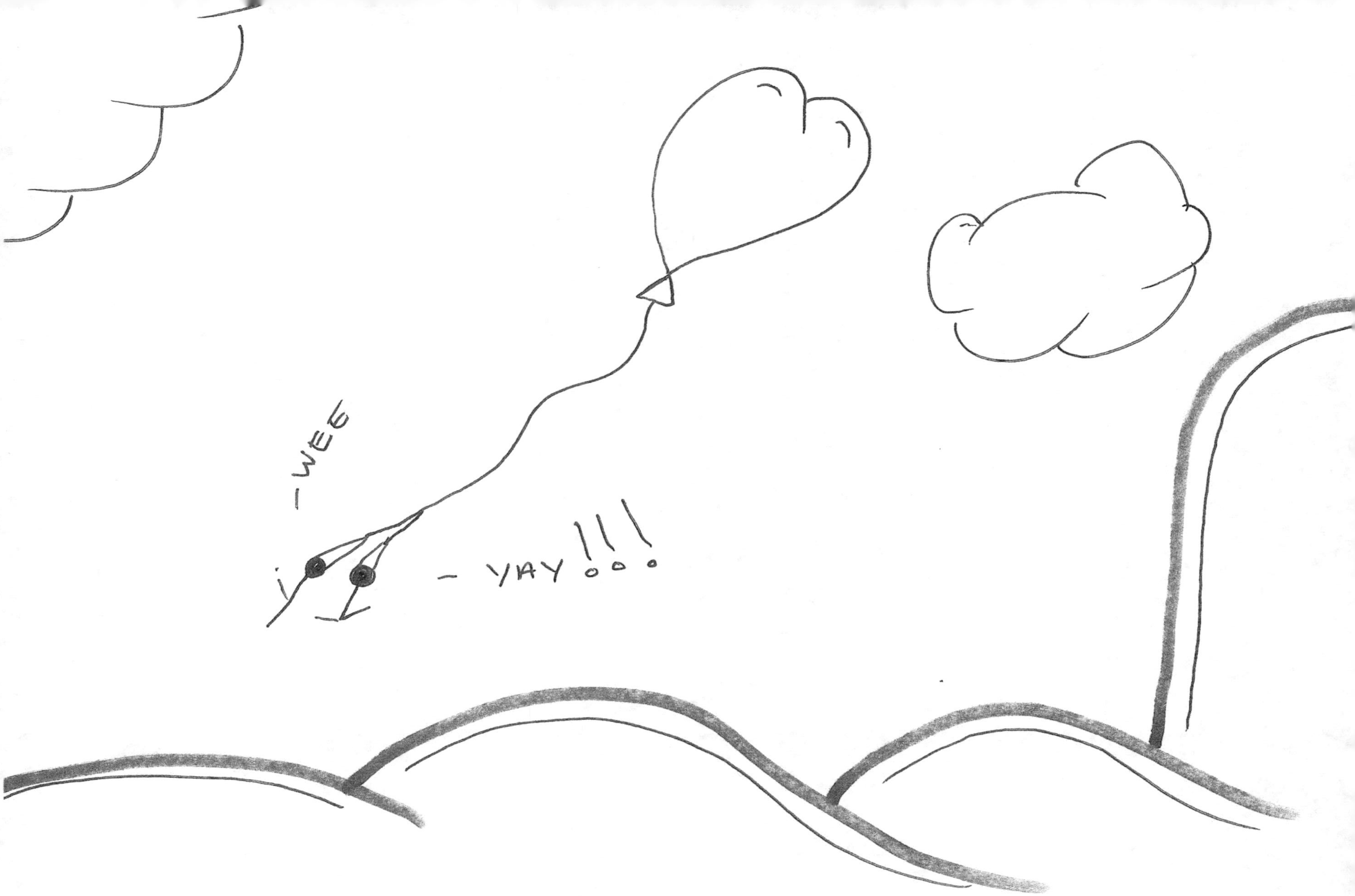
-WEE
- YAY!!!

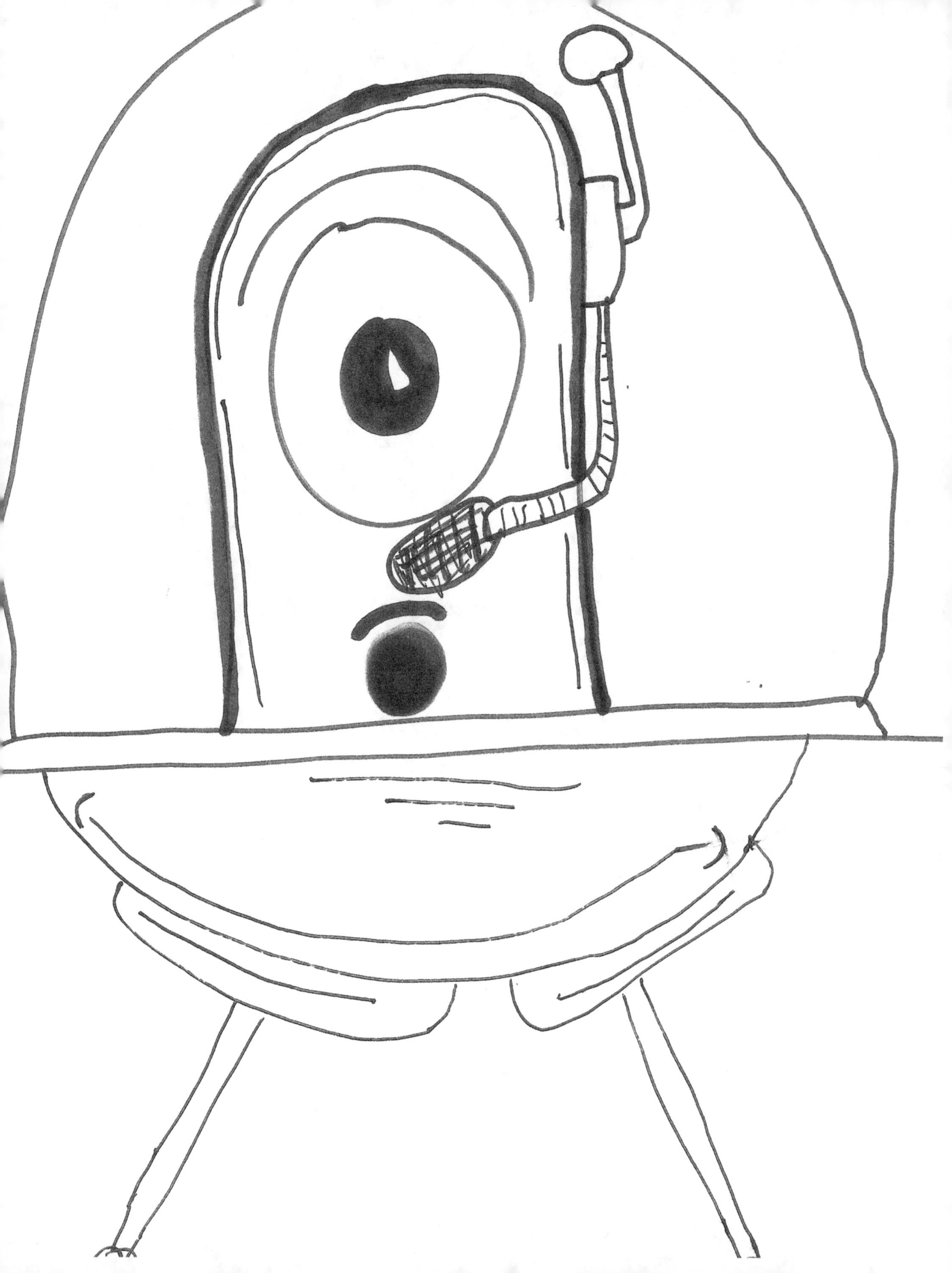

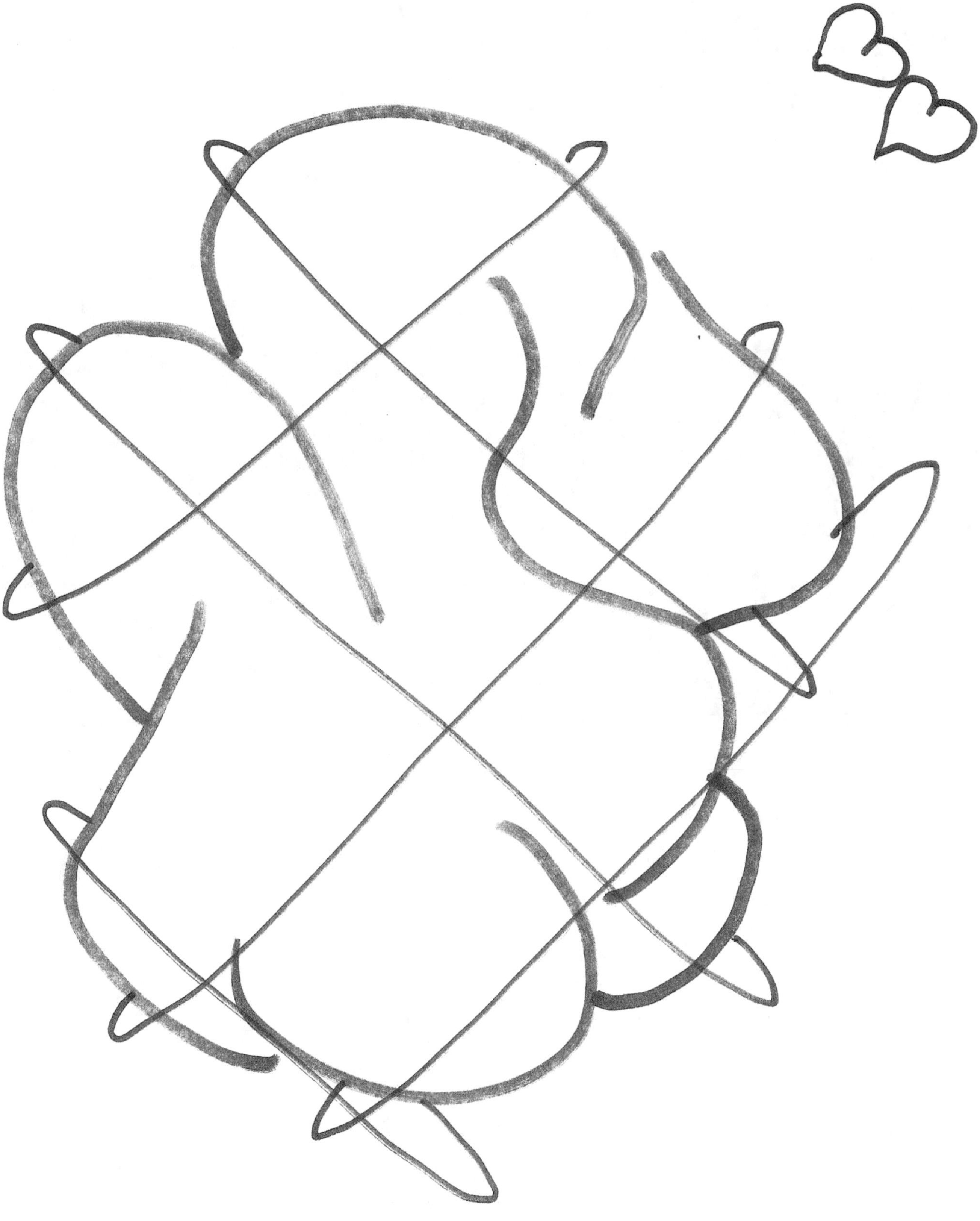

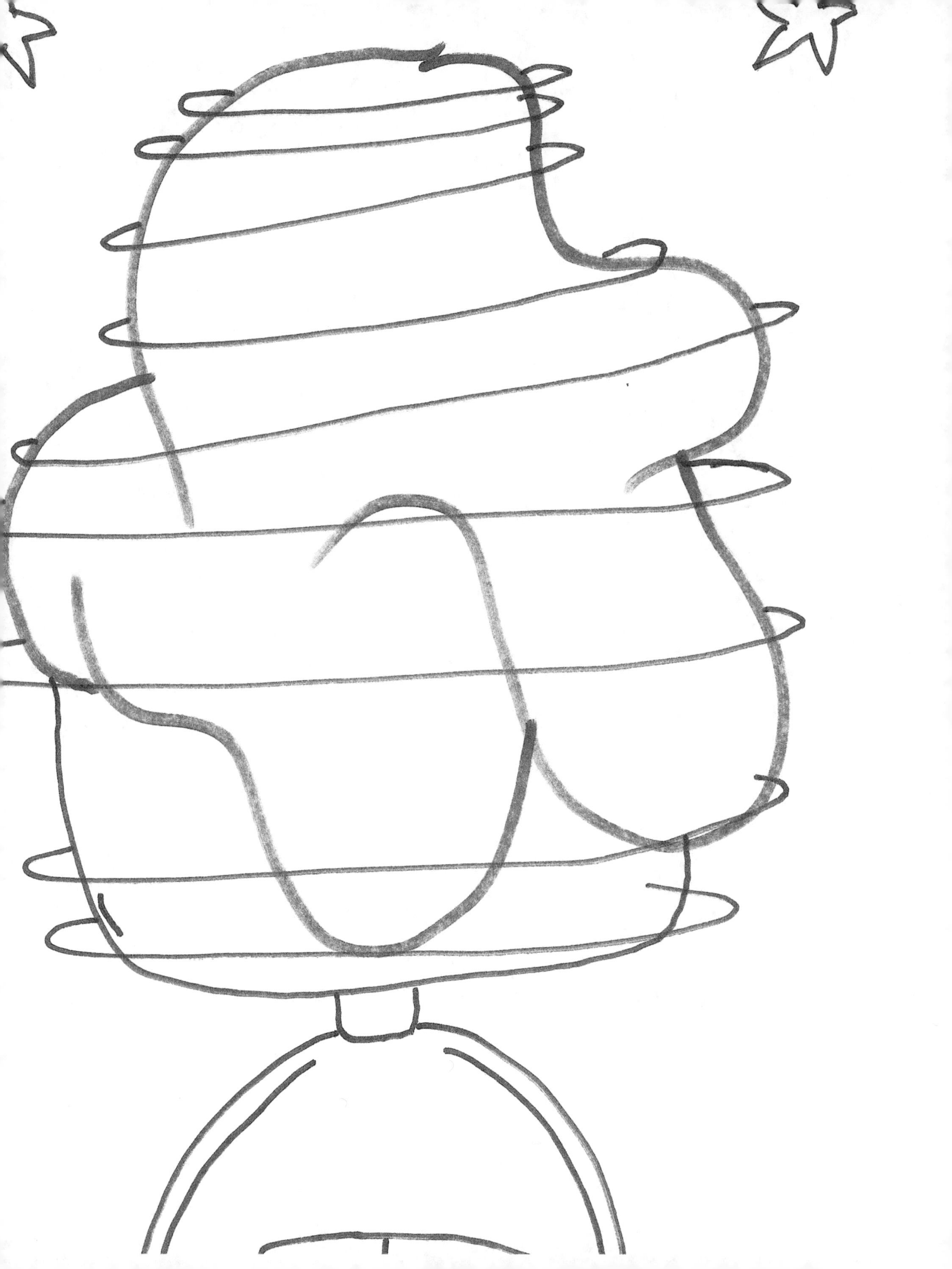

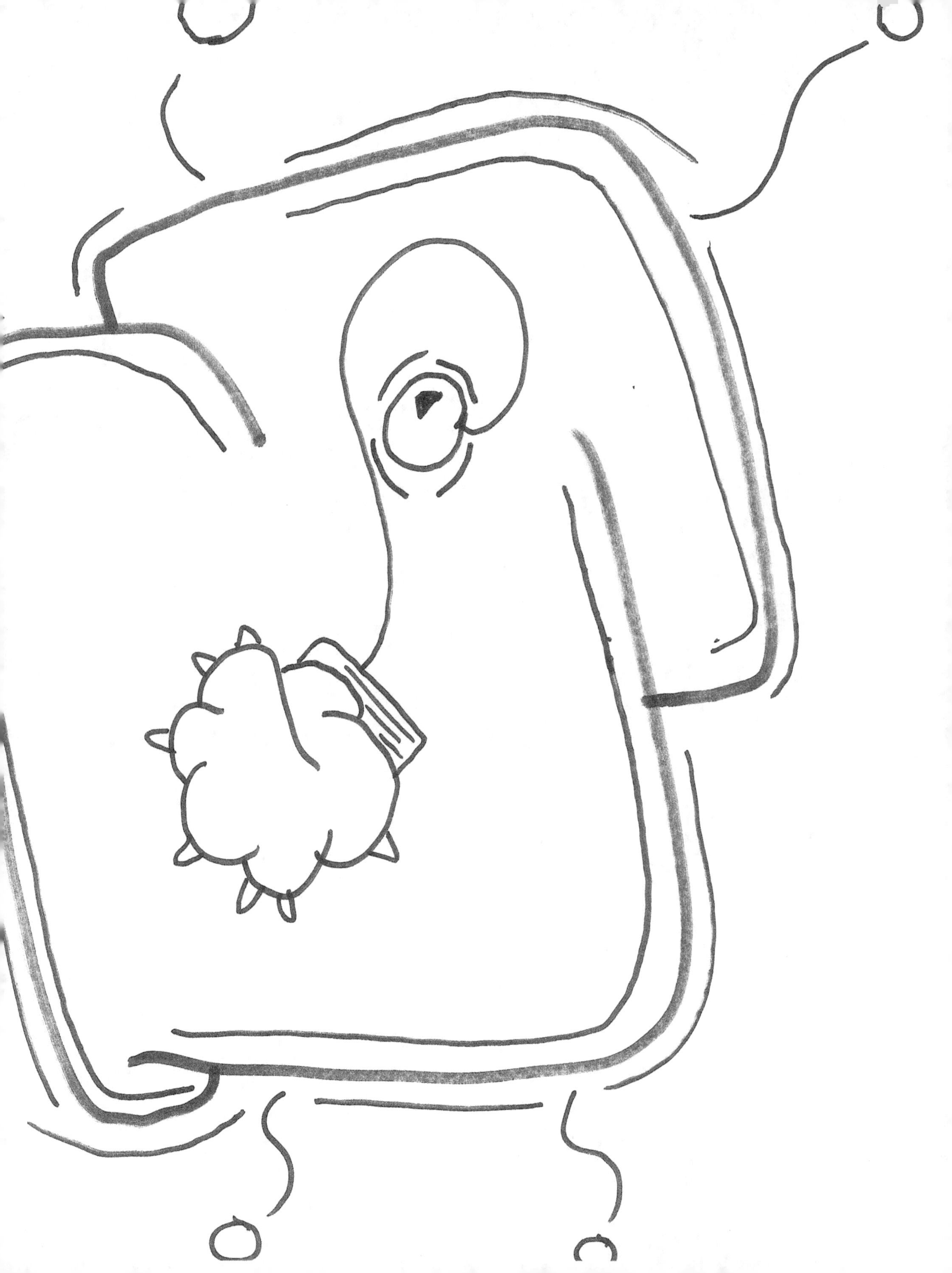

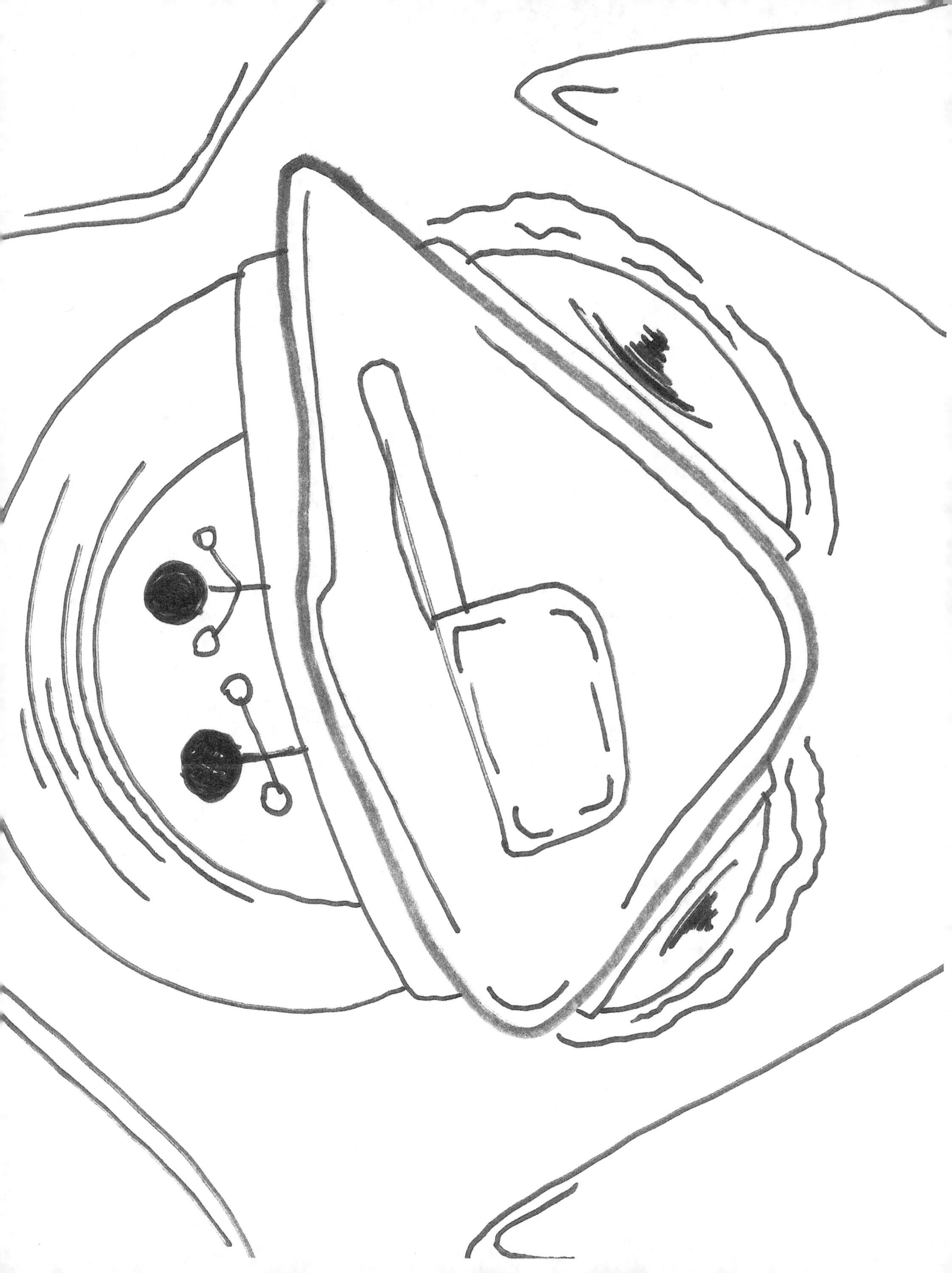

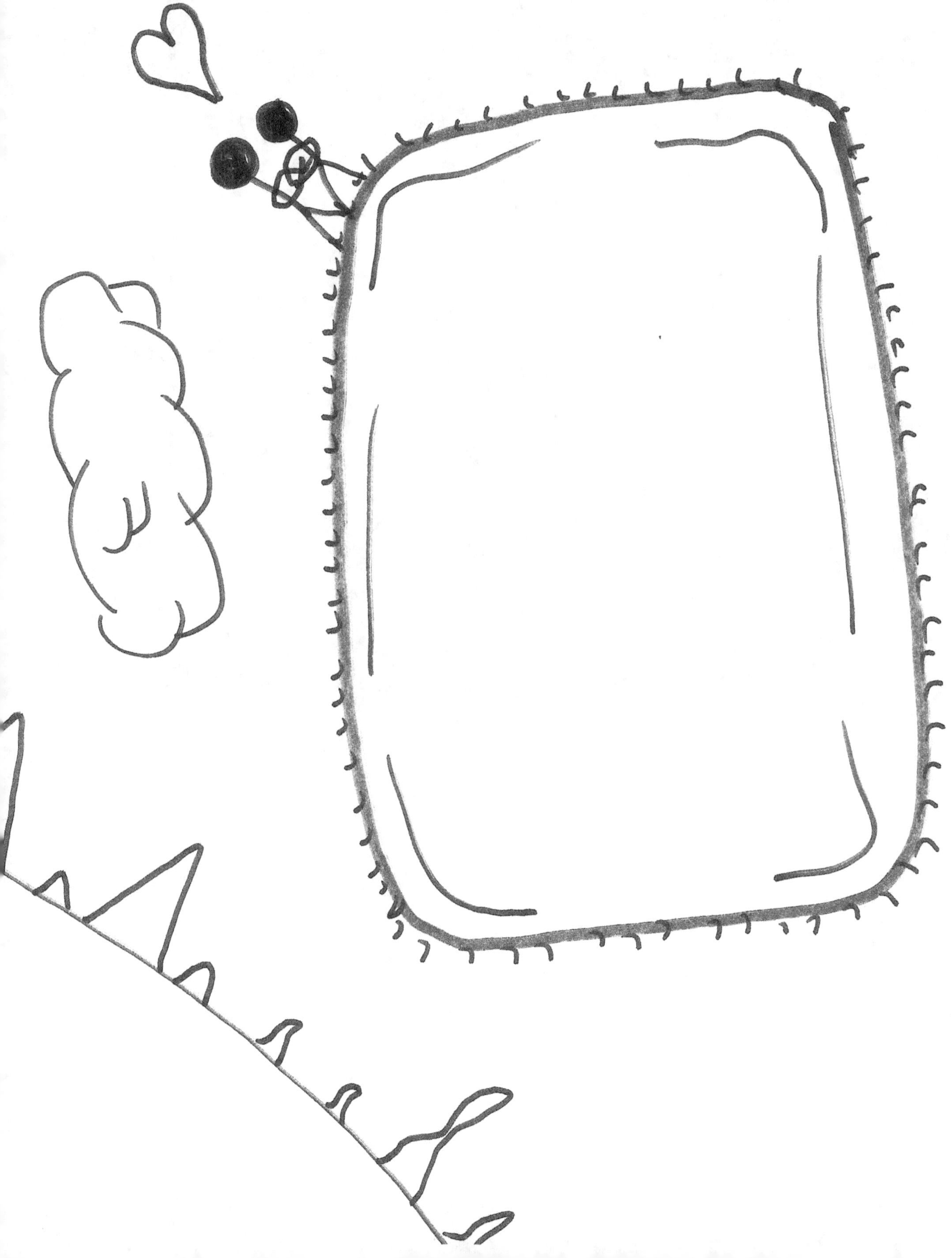

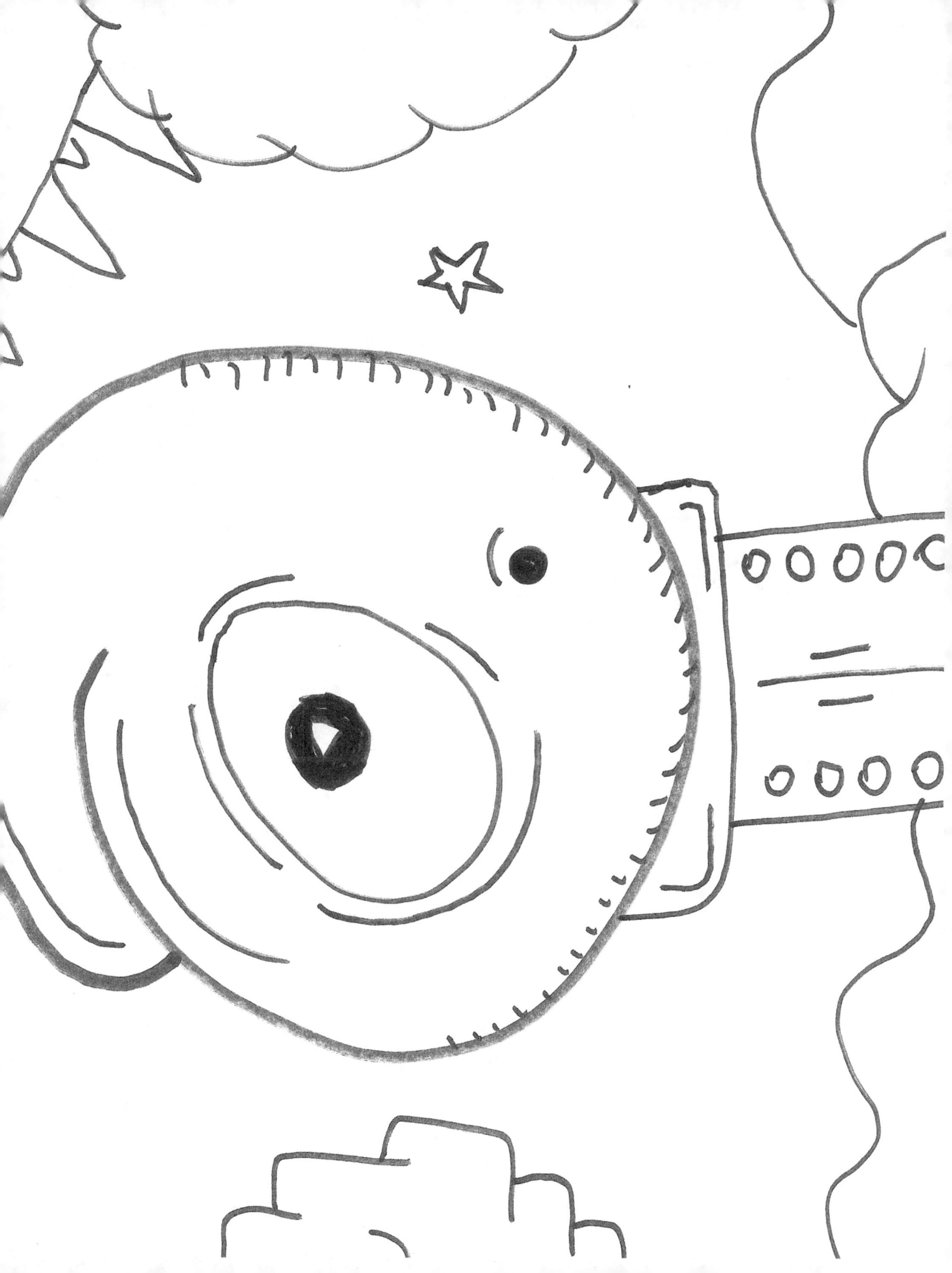

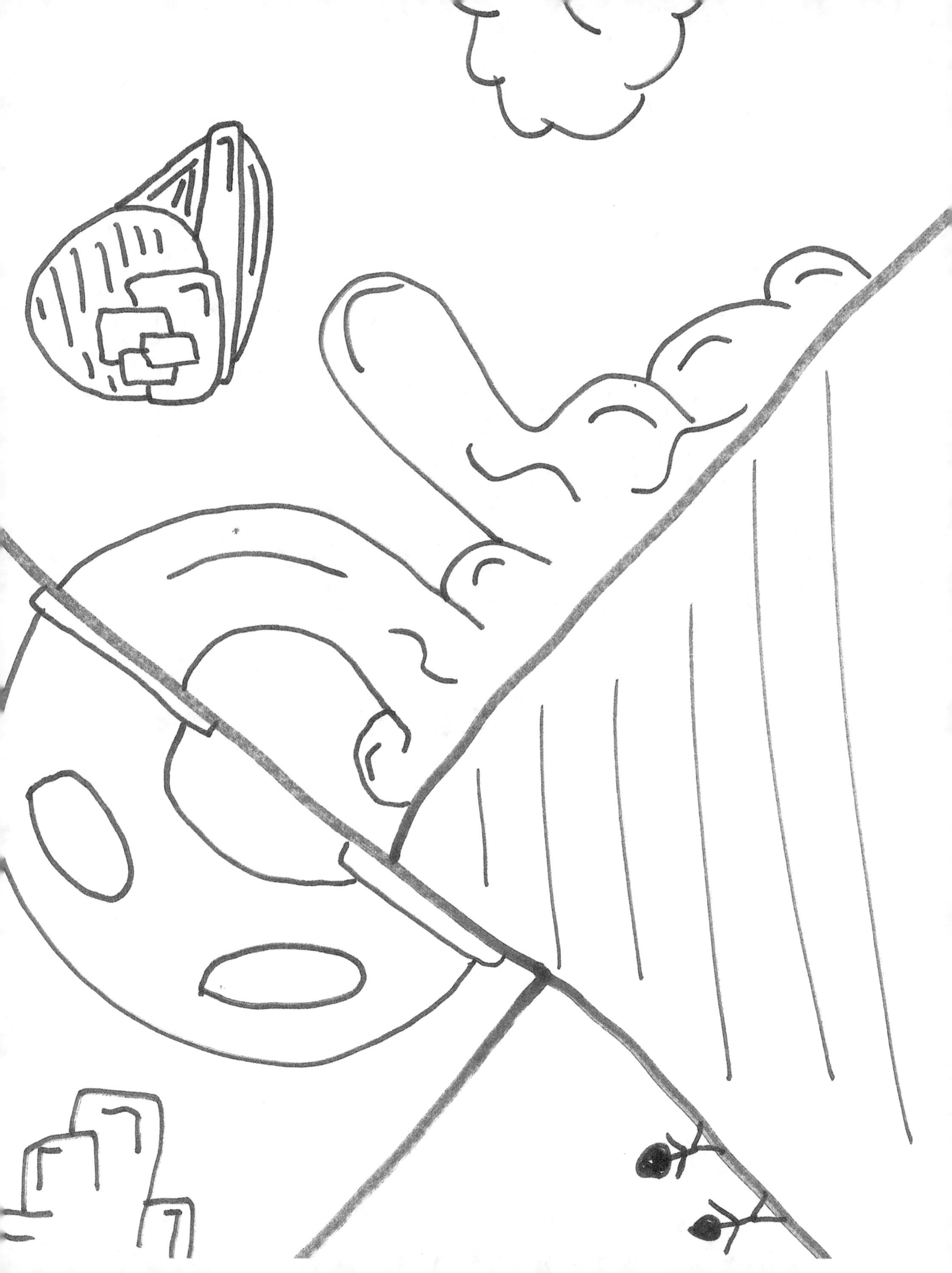

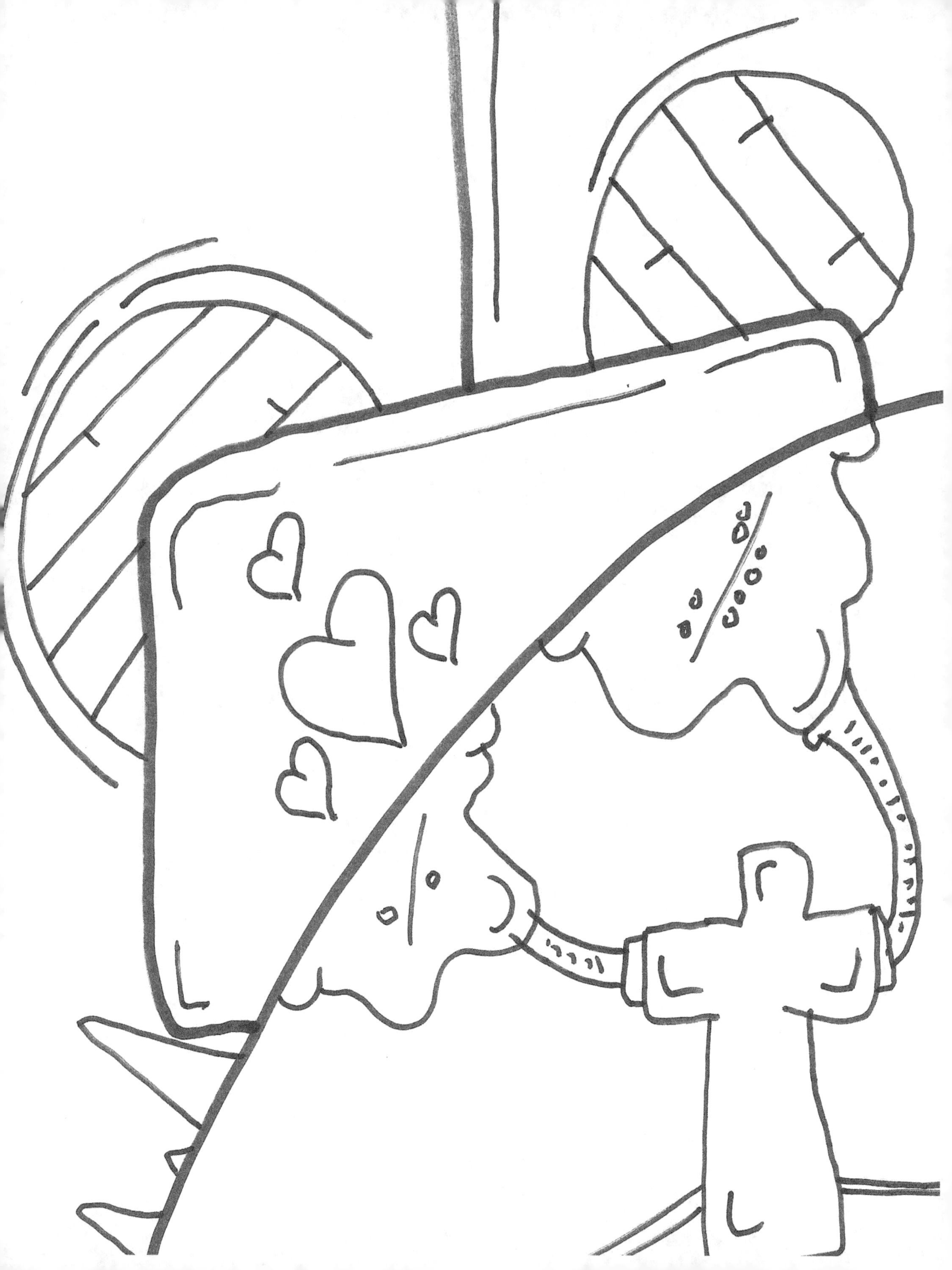

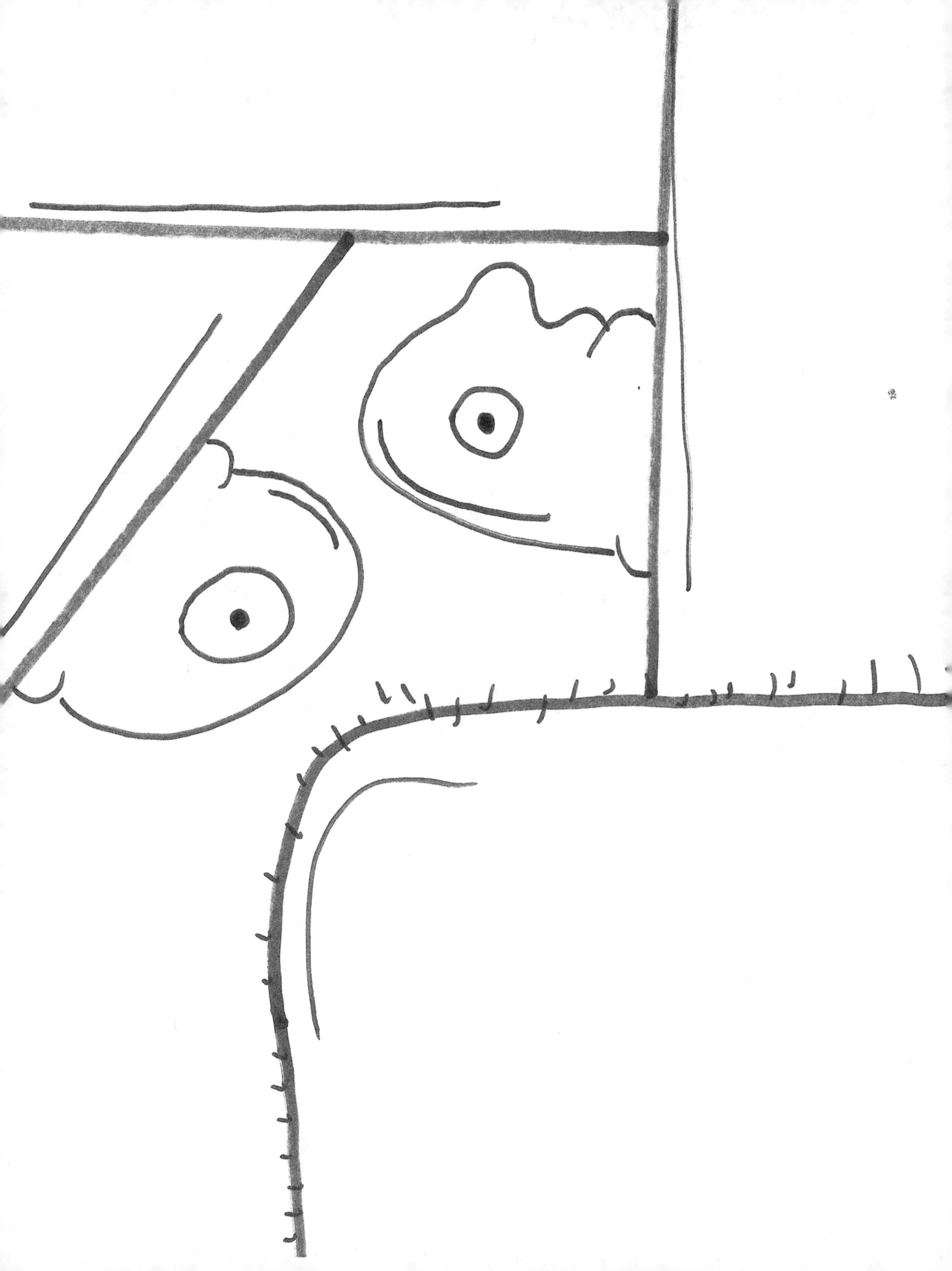

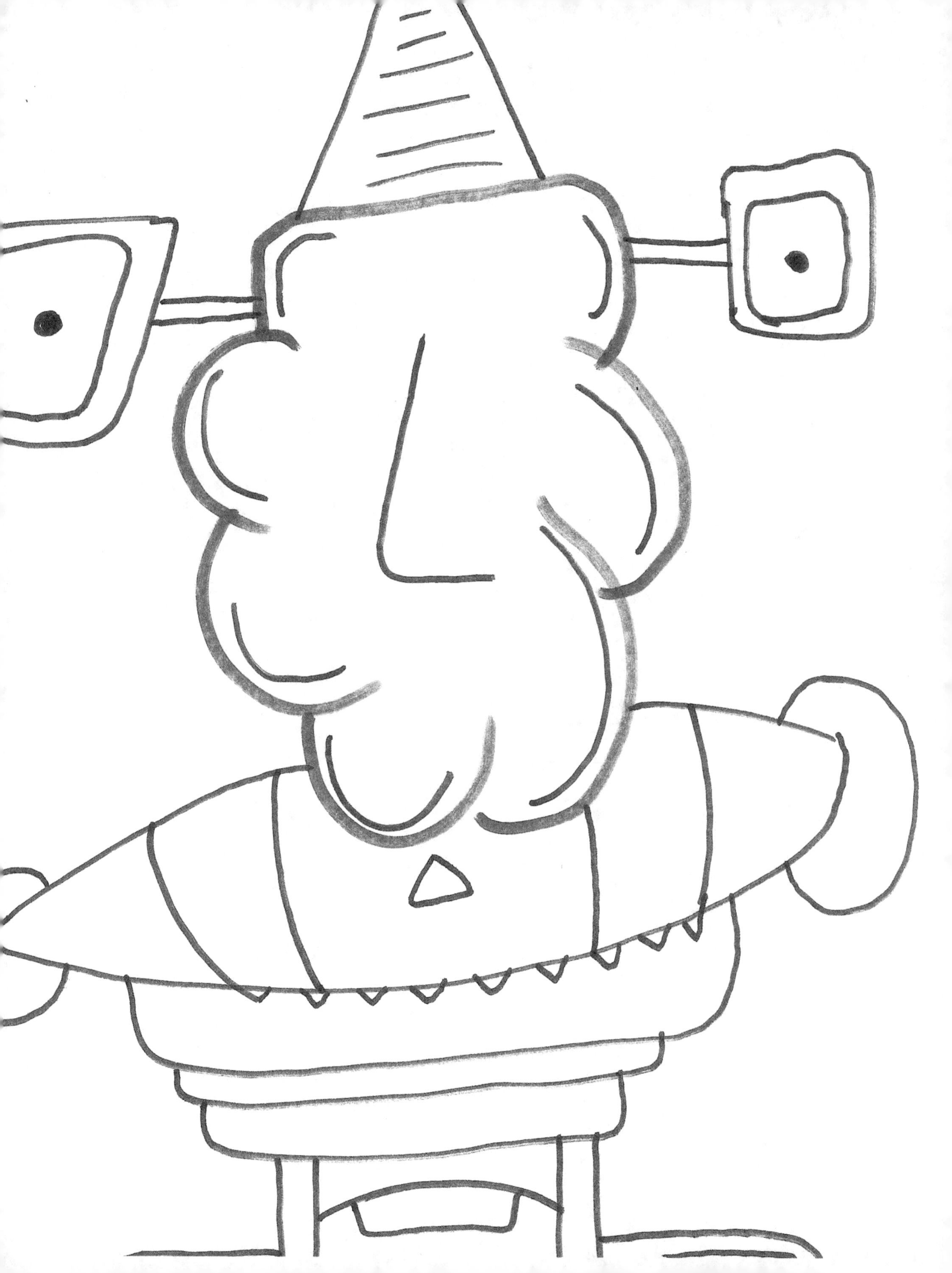

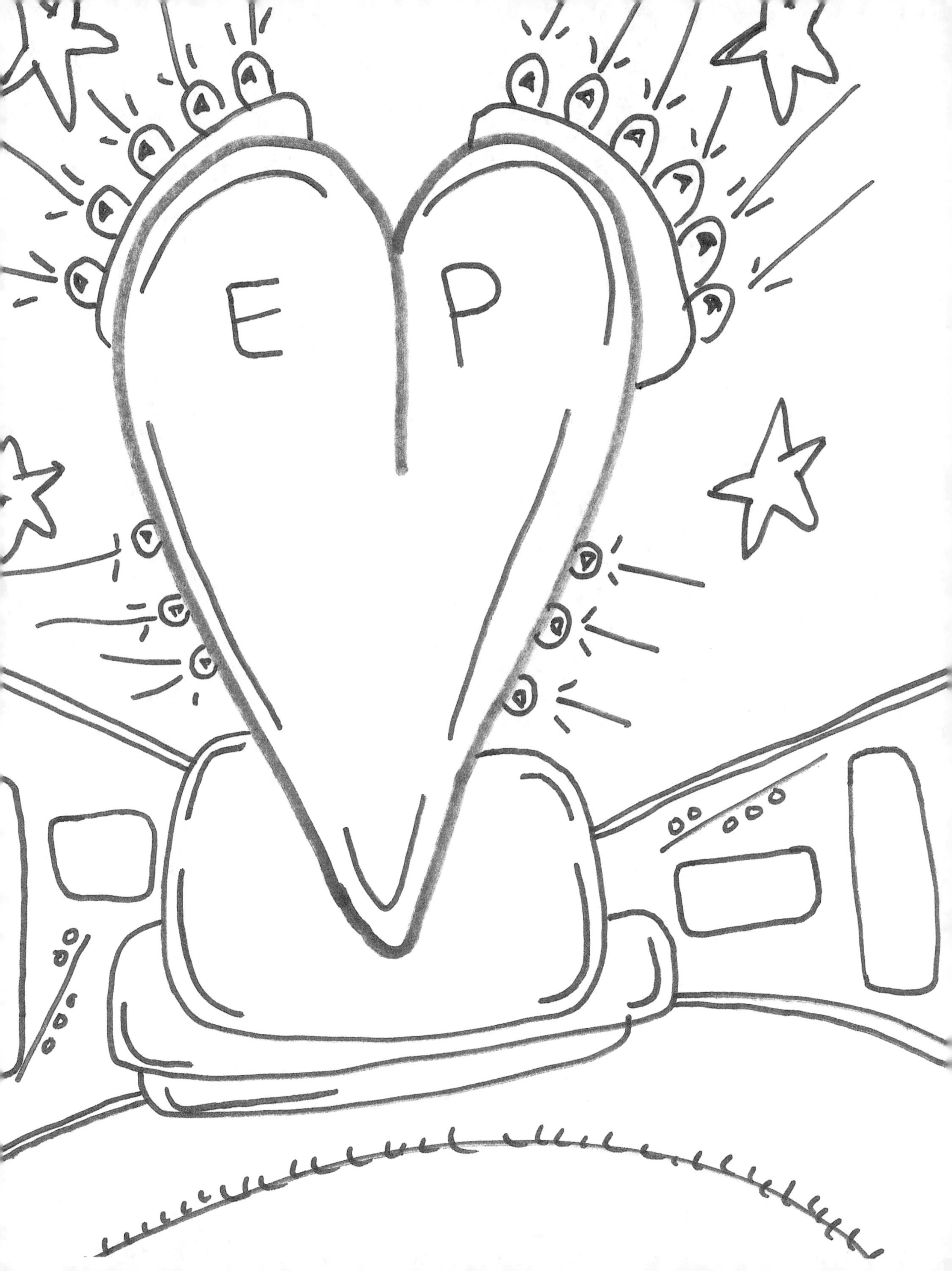
E P

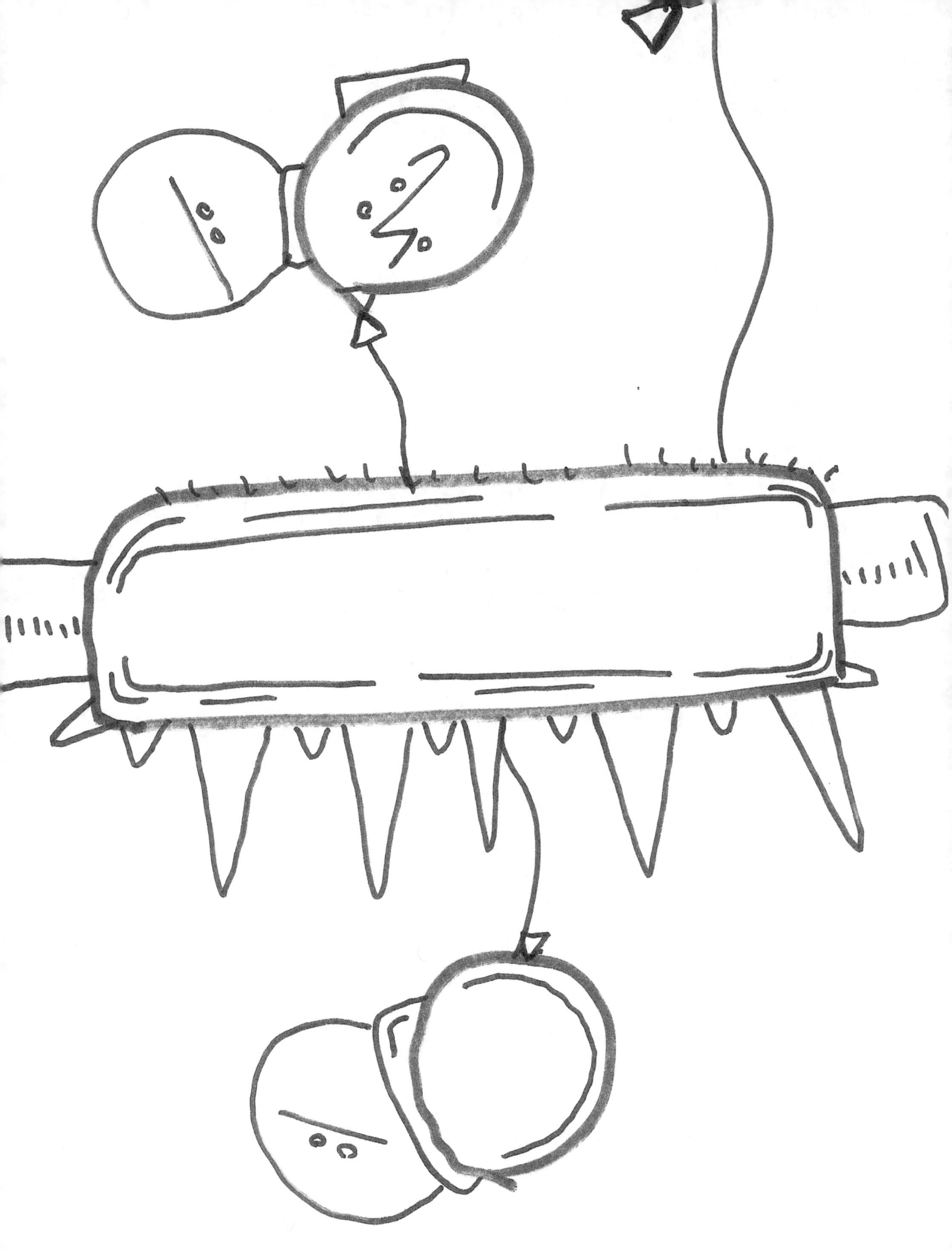

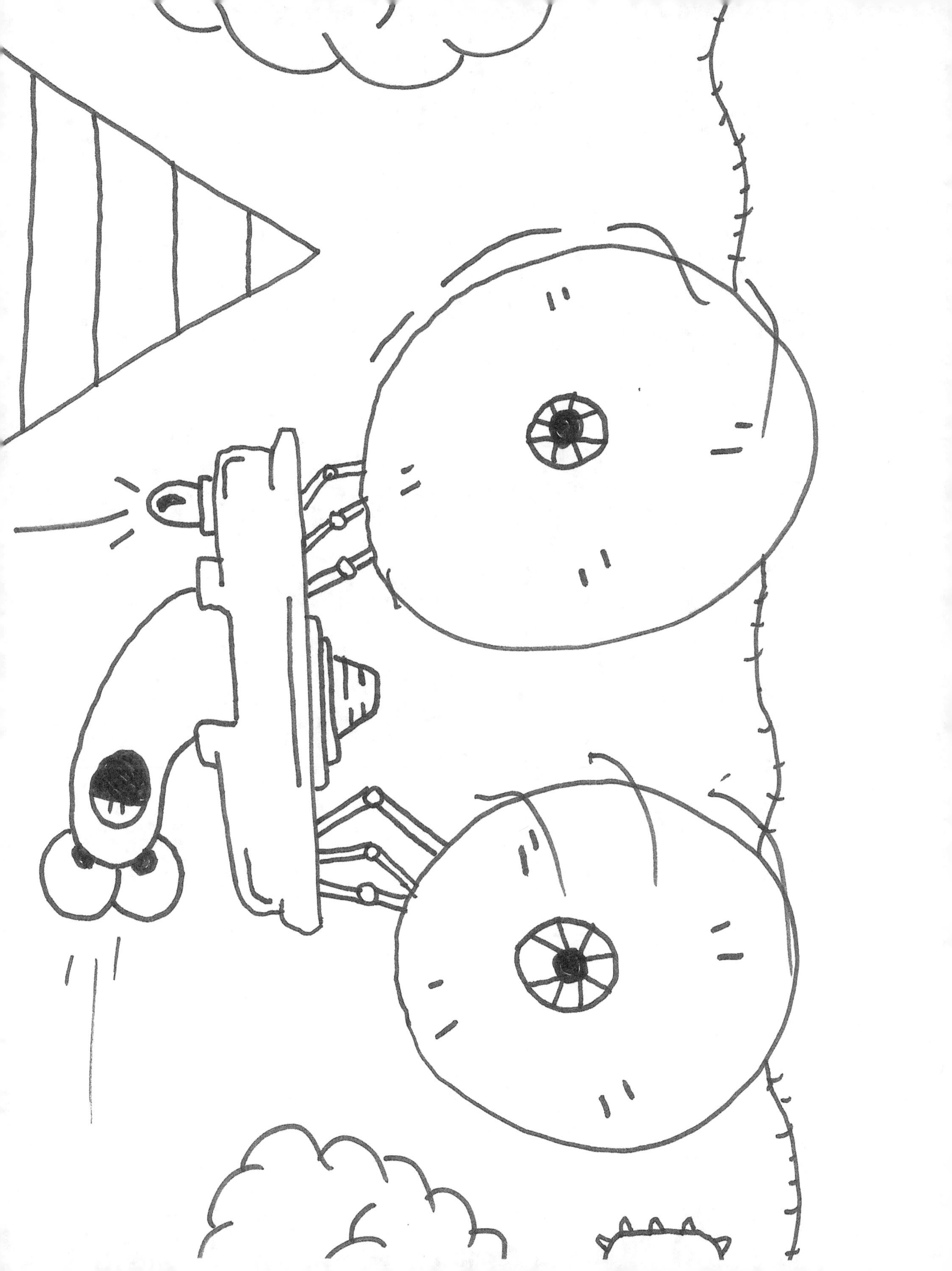

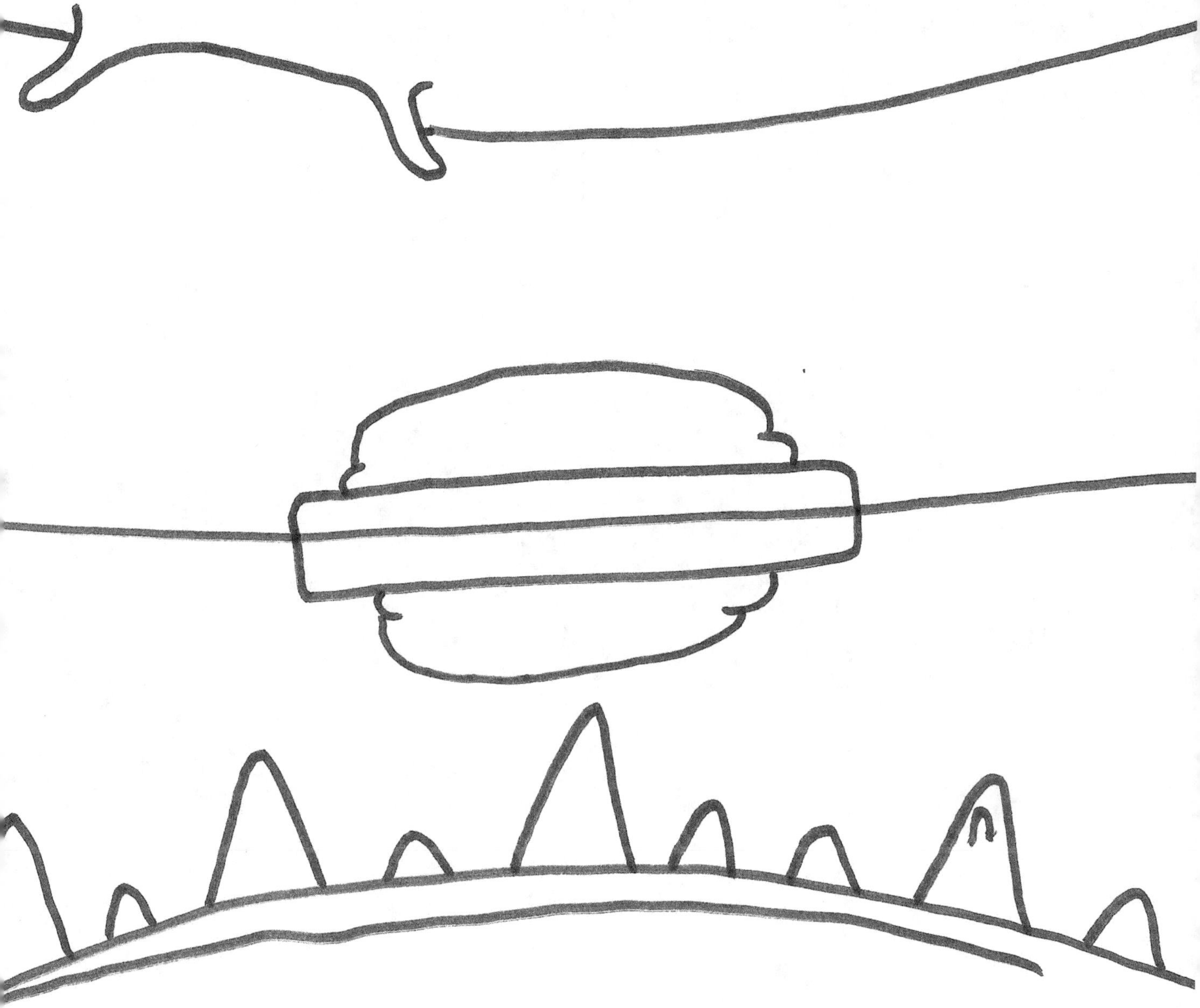

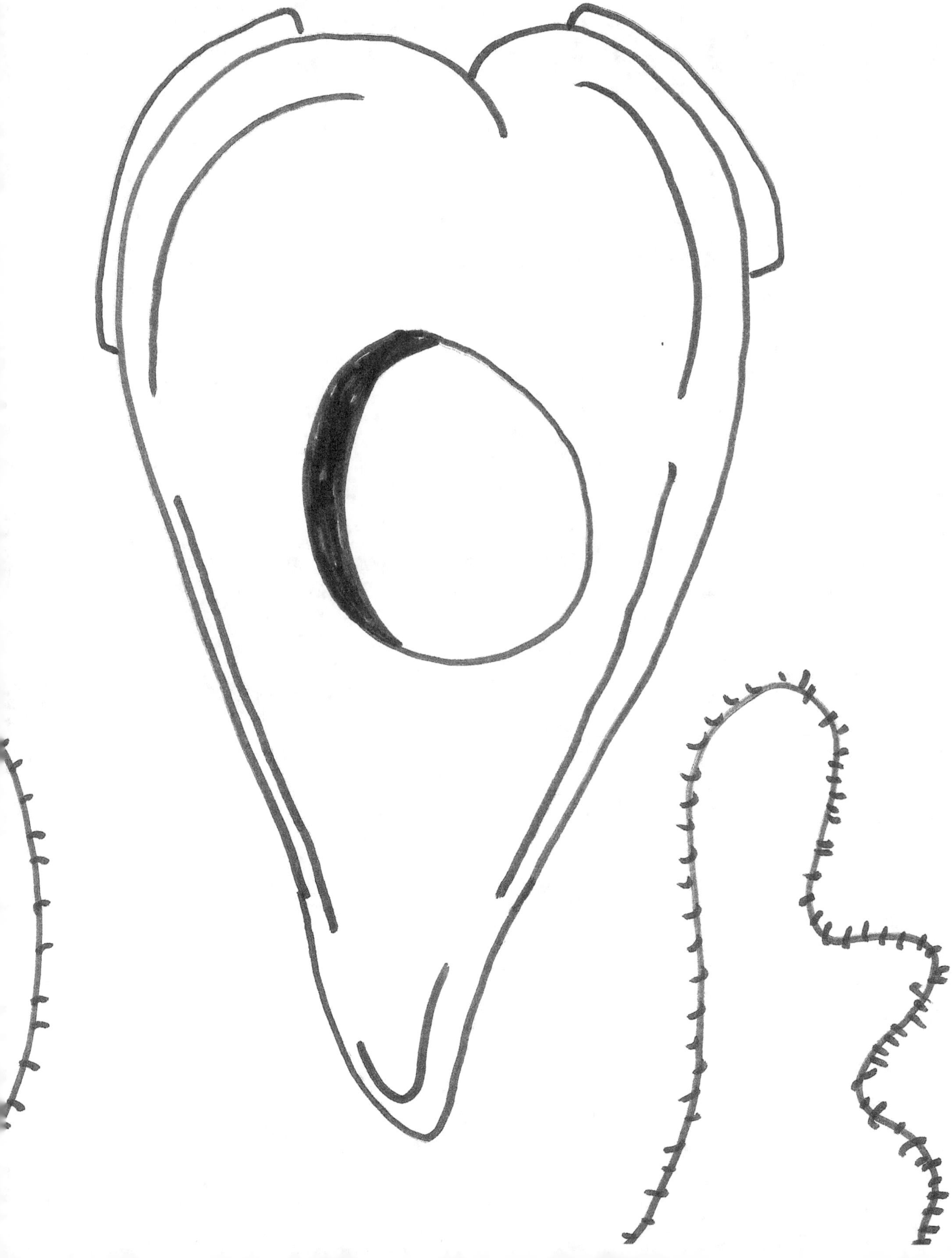

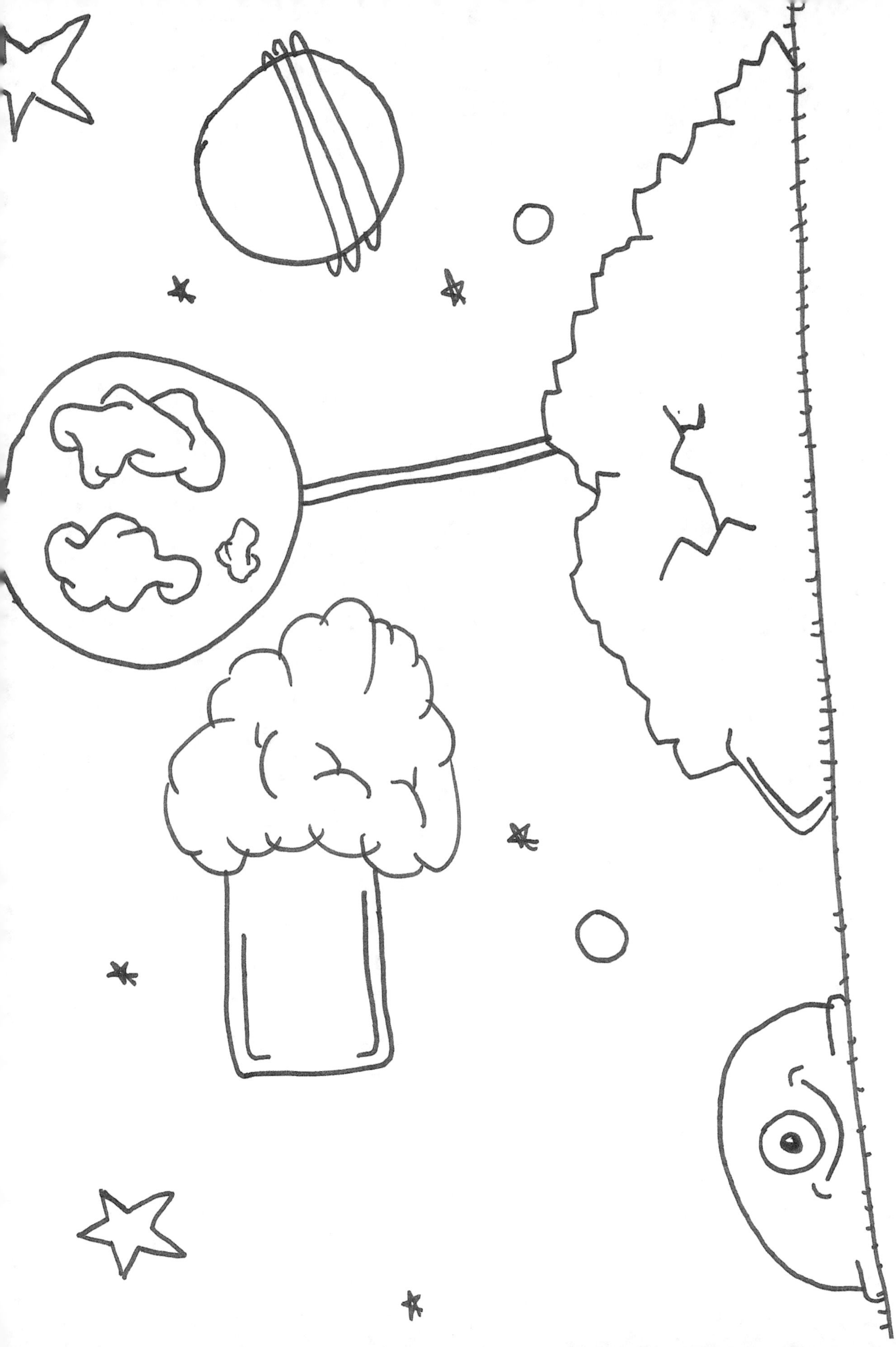

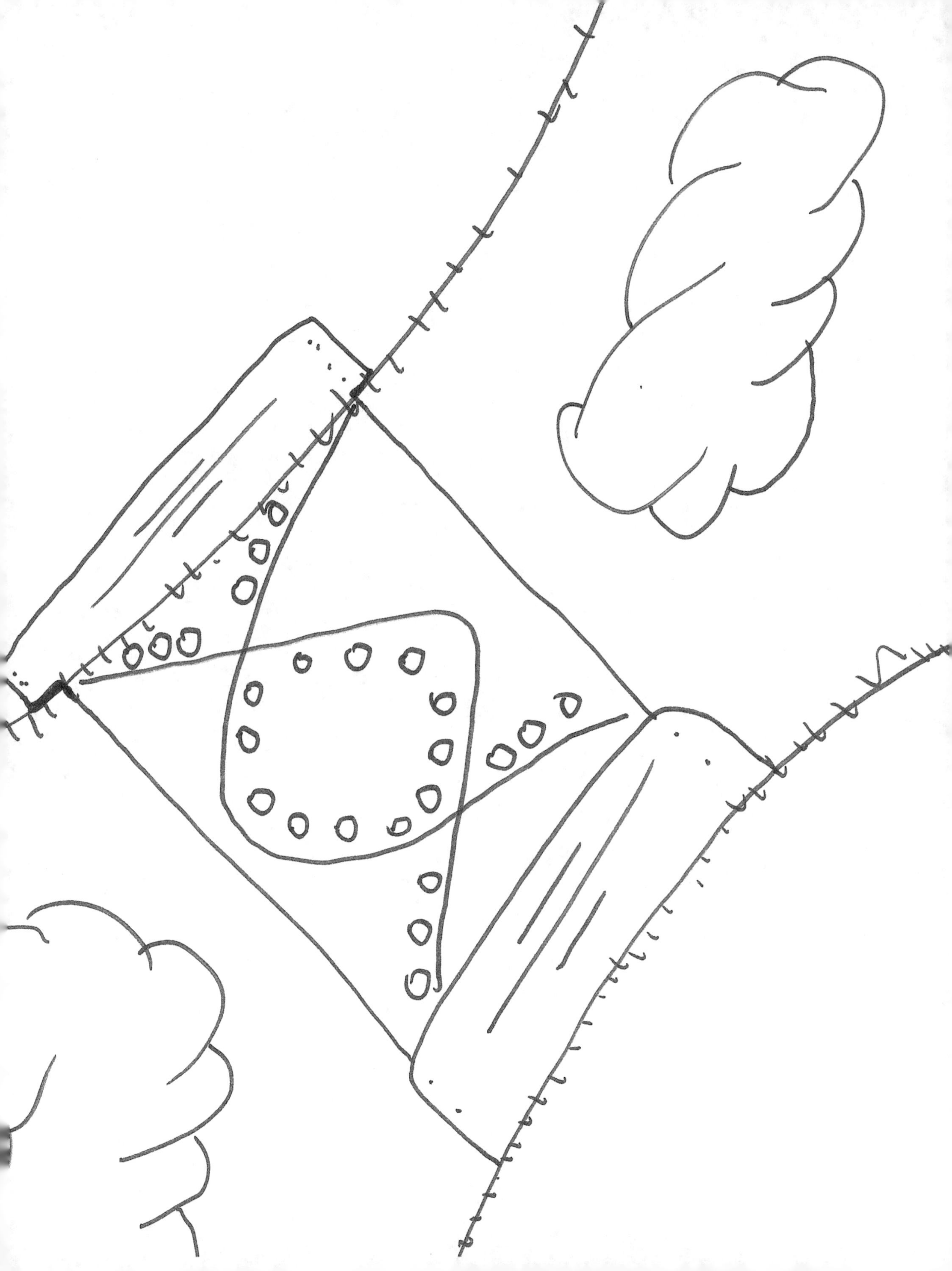

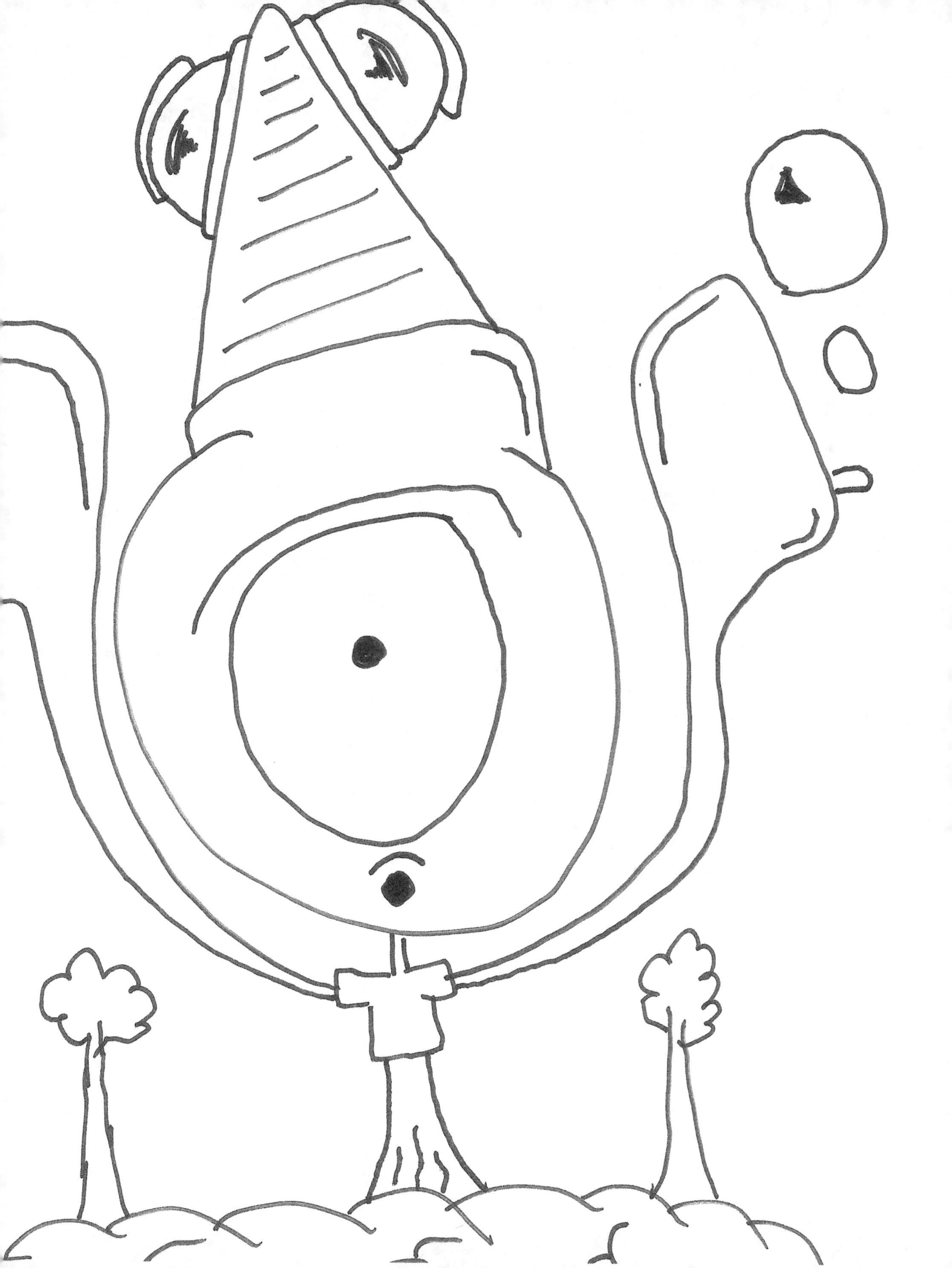

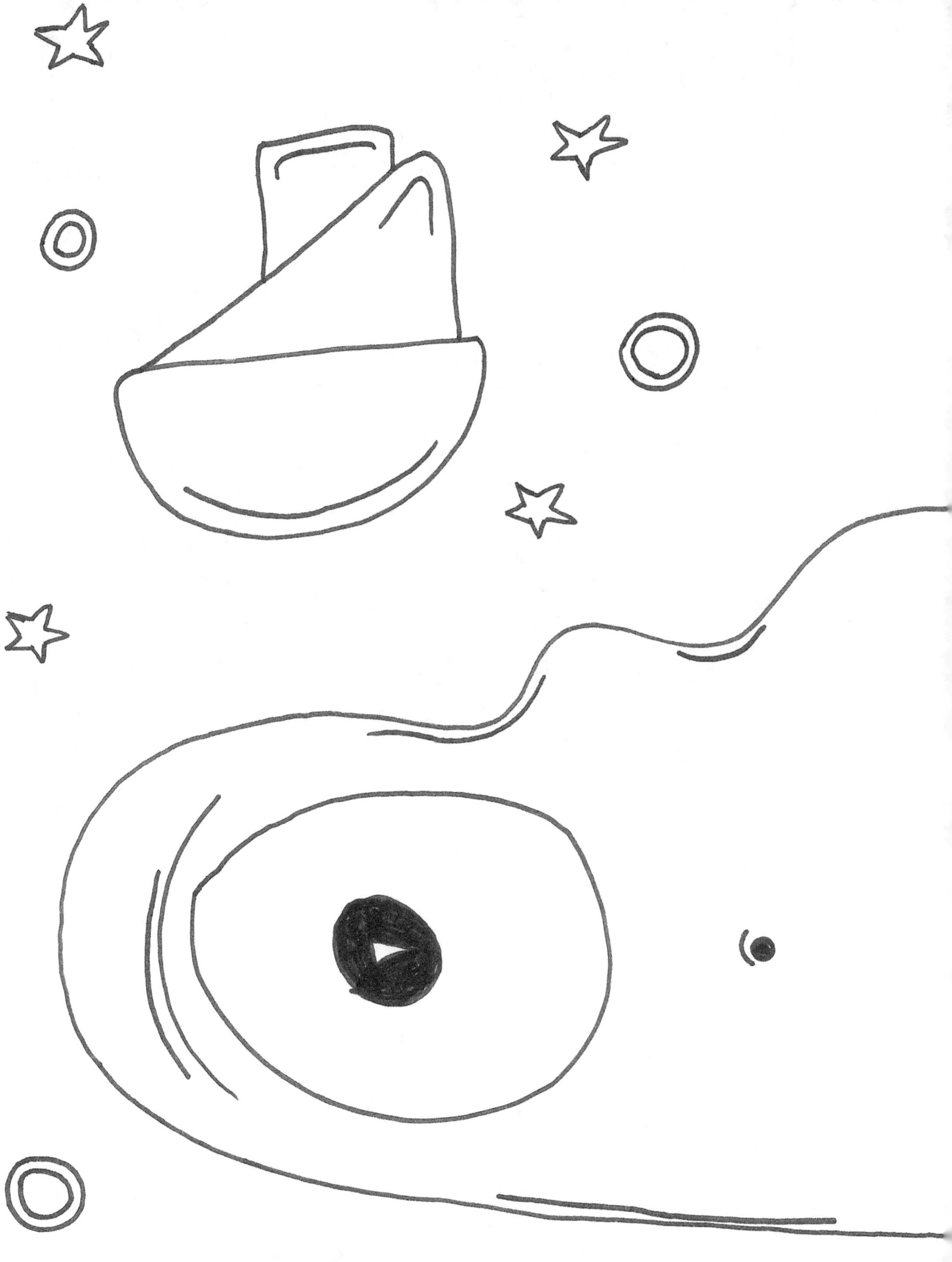

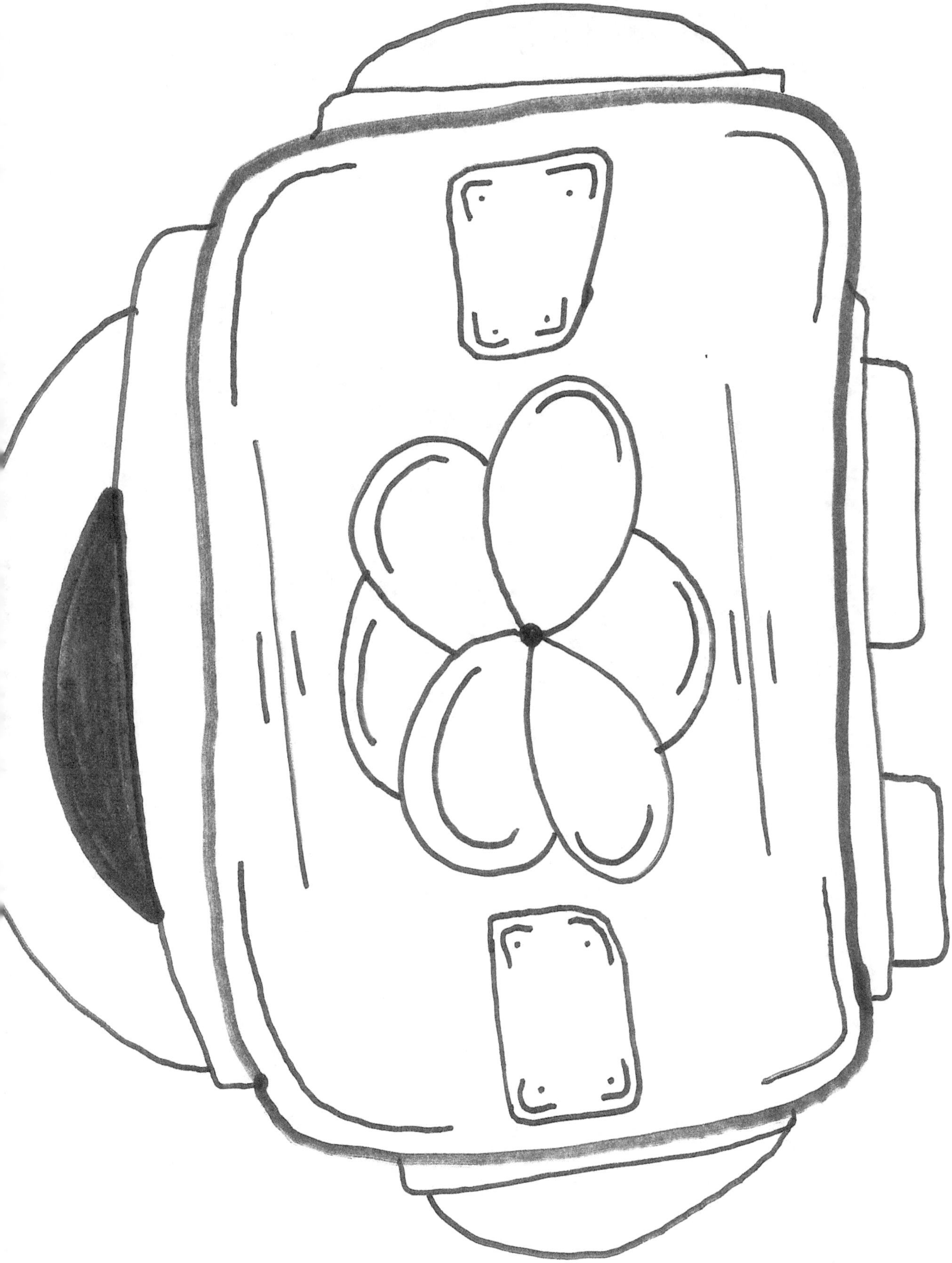

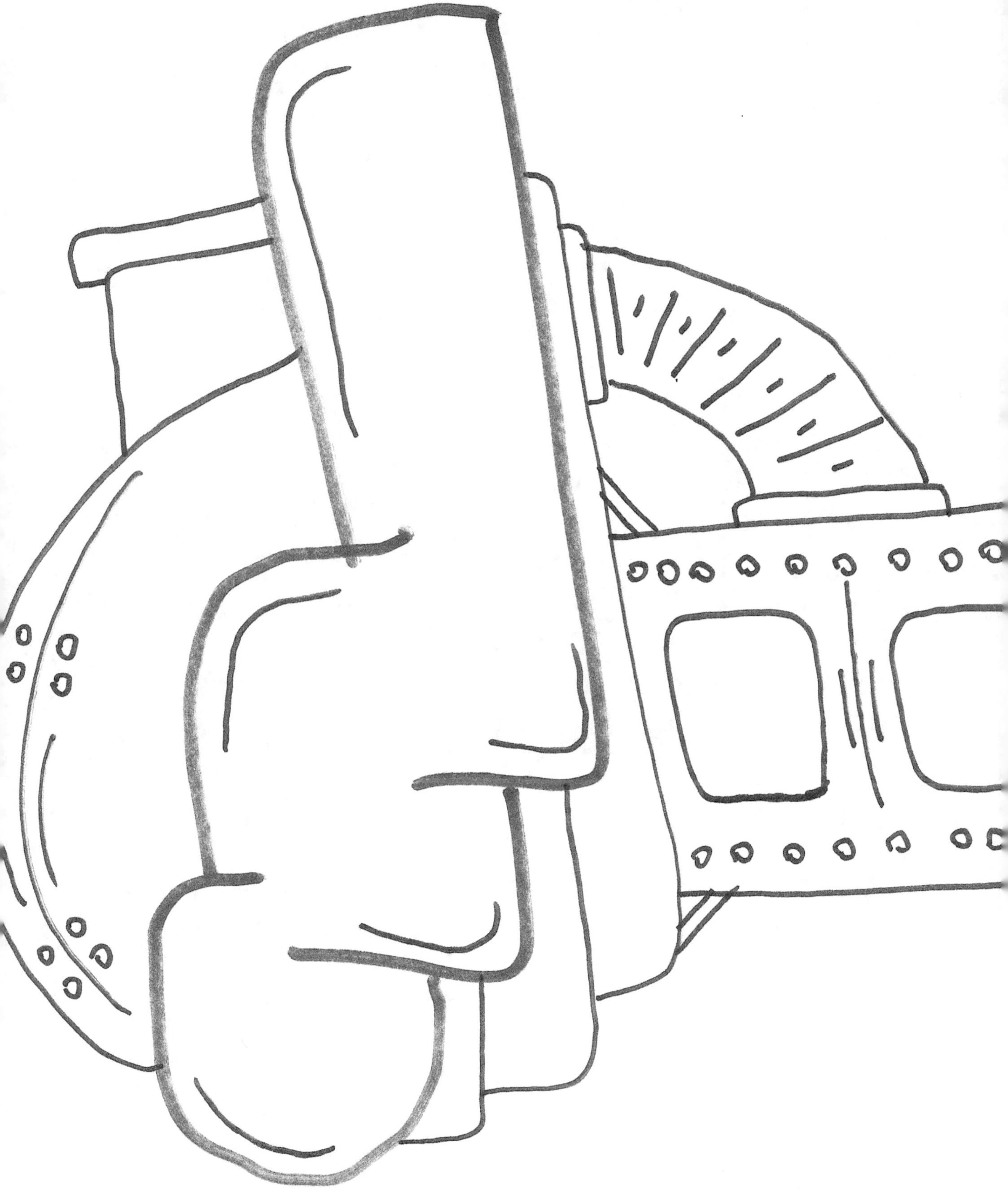

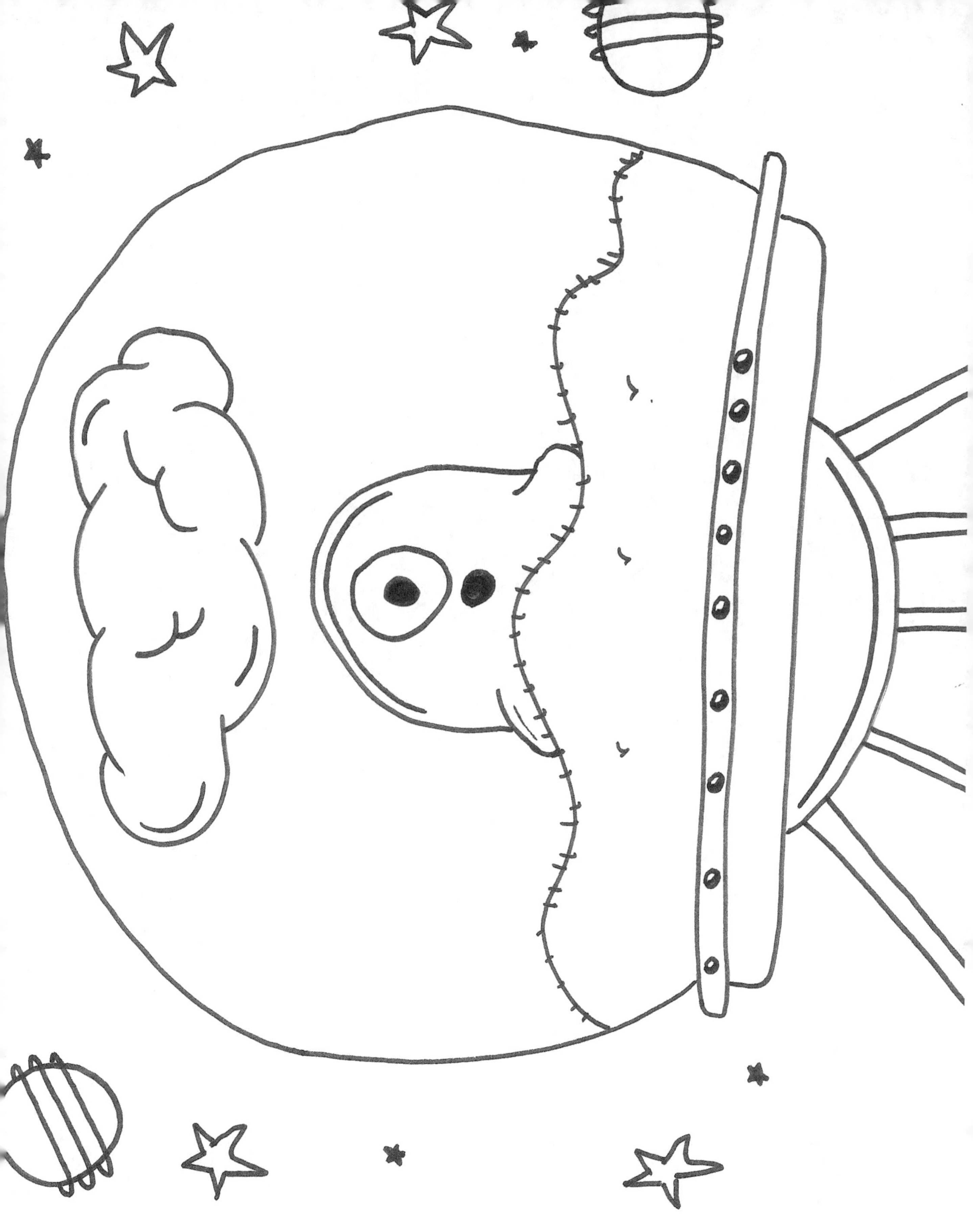

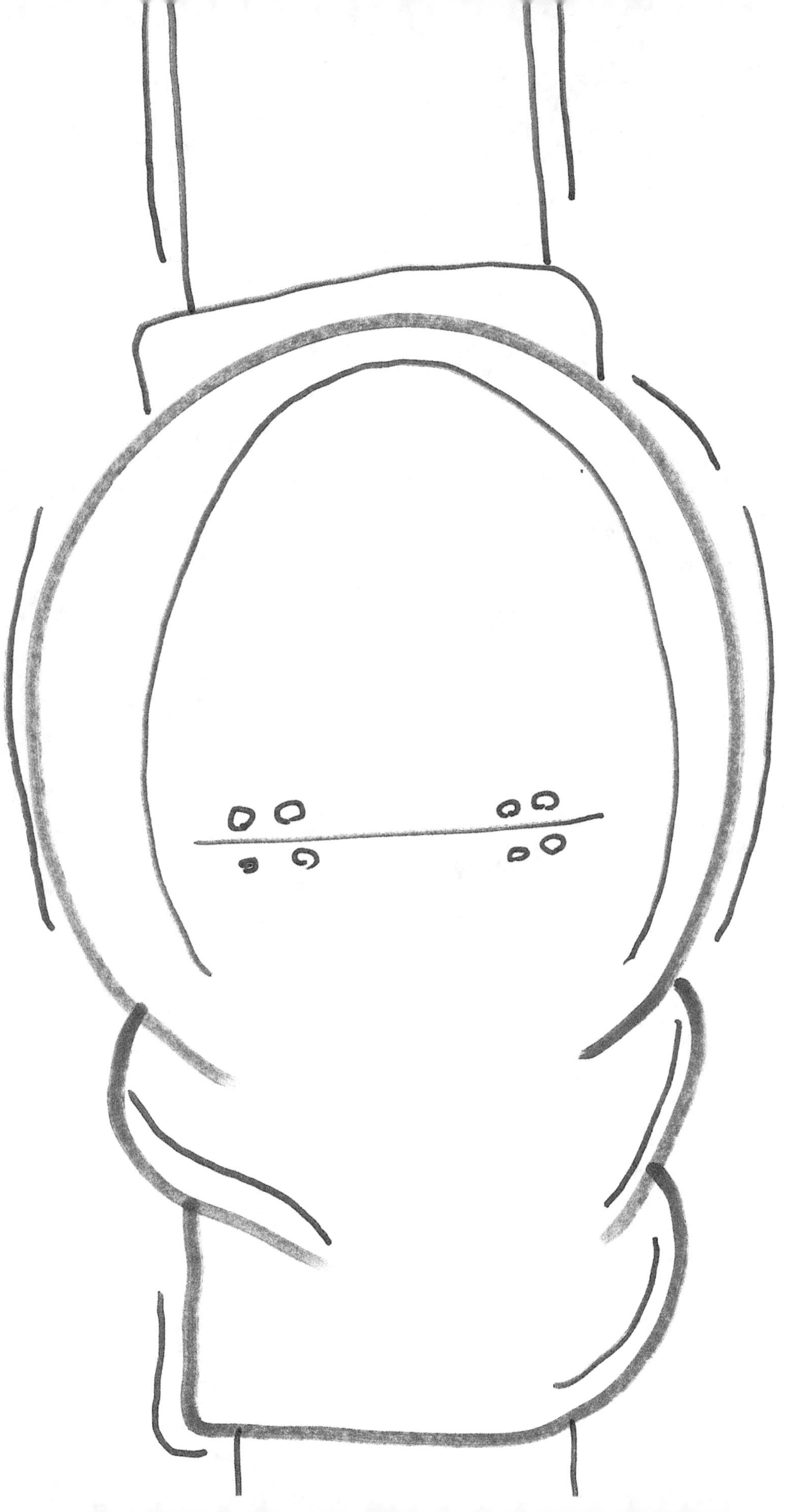

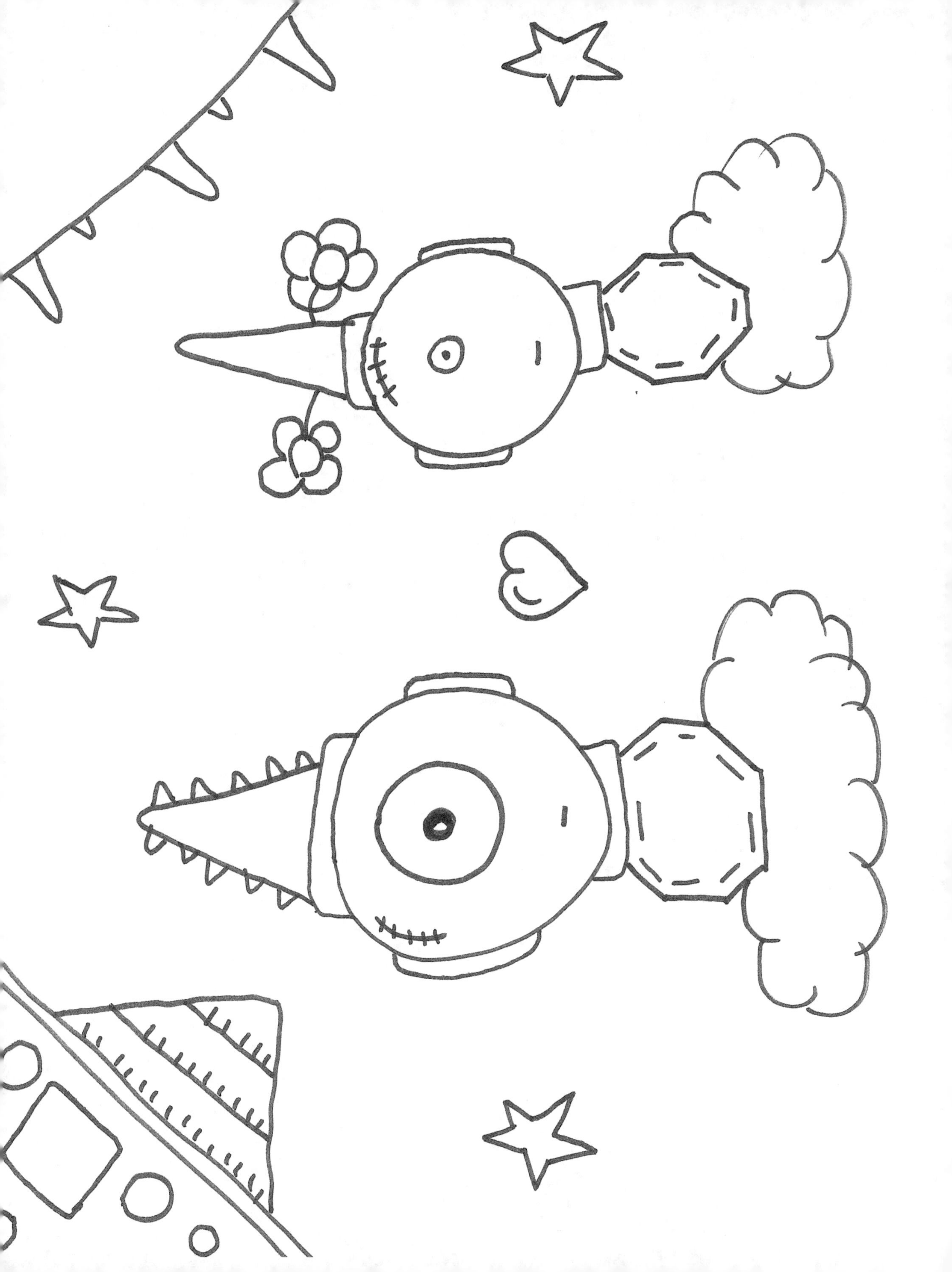

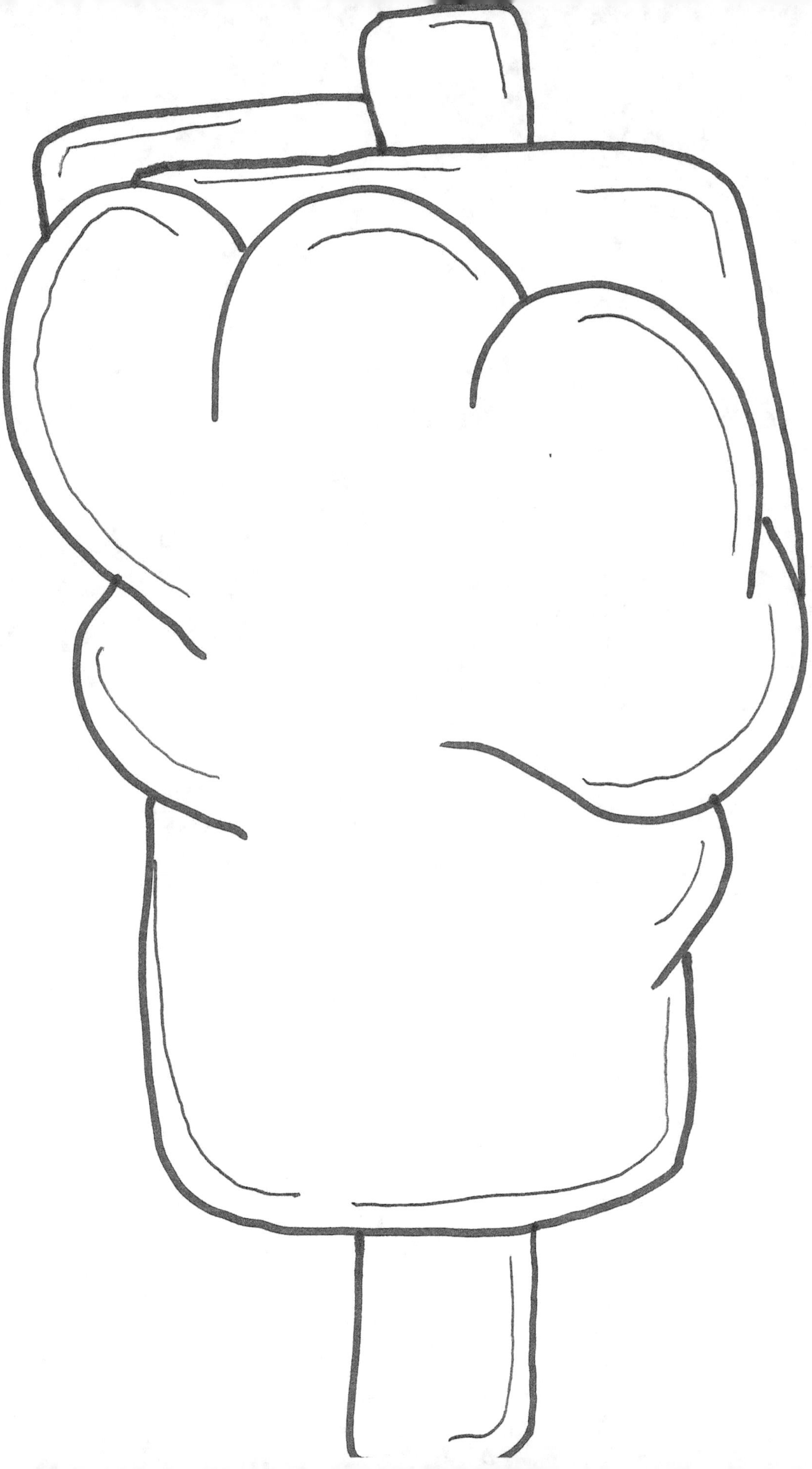

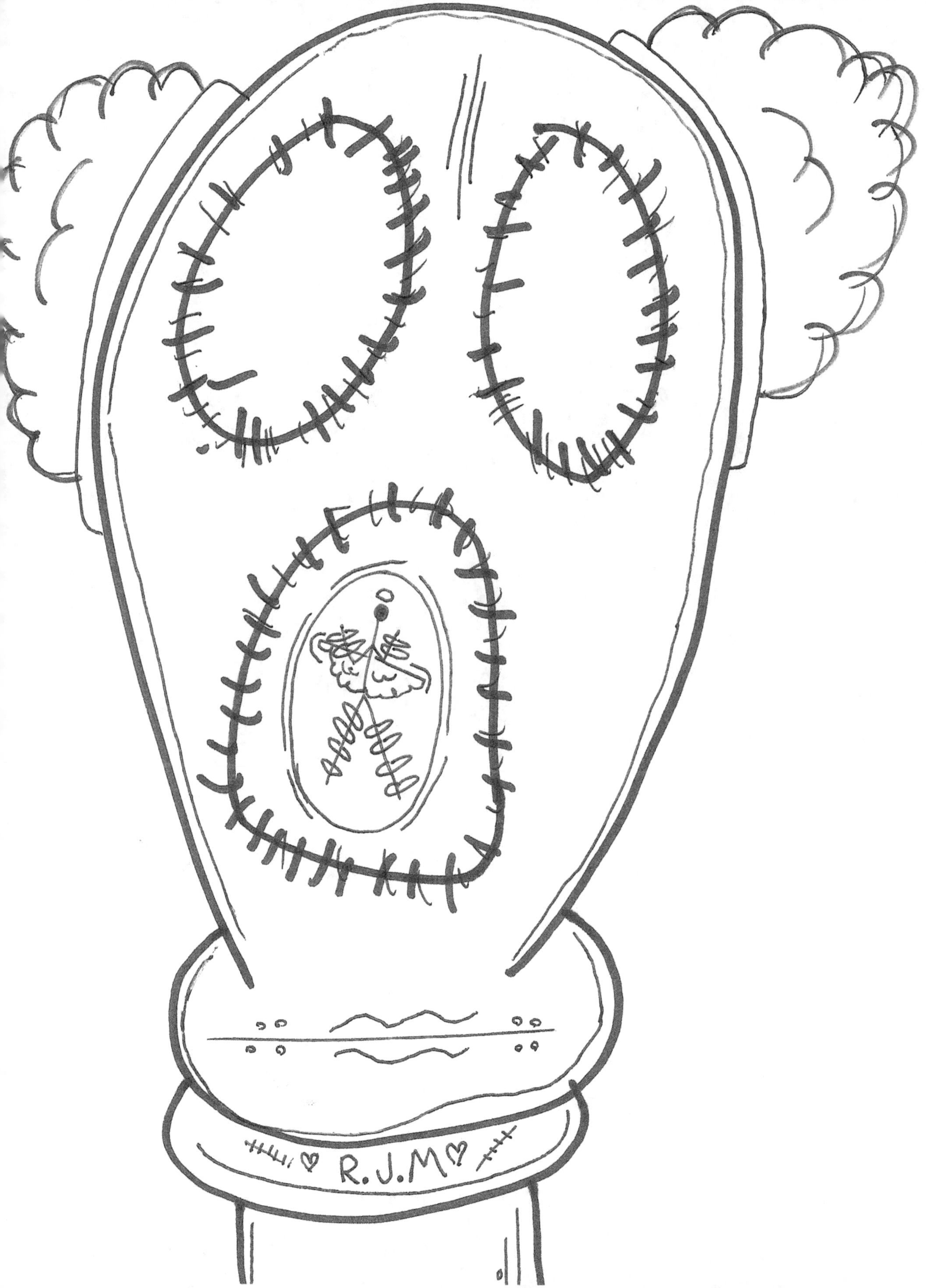
R.J.M

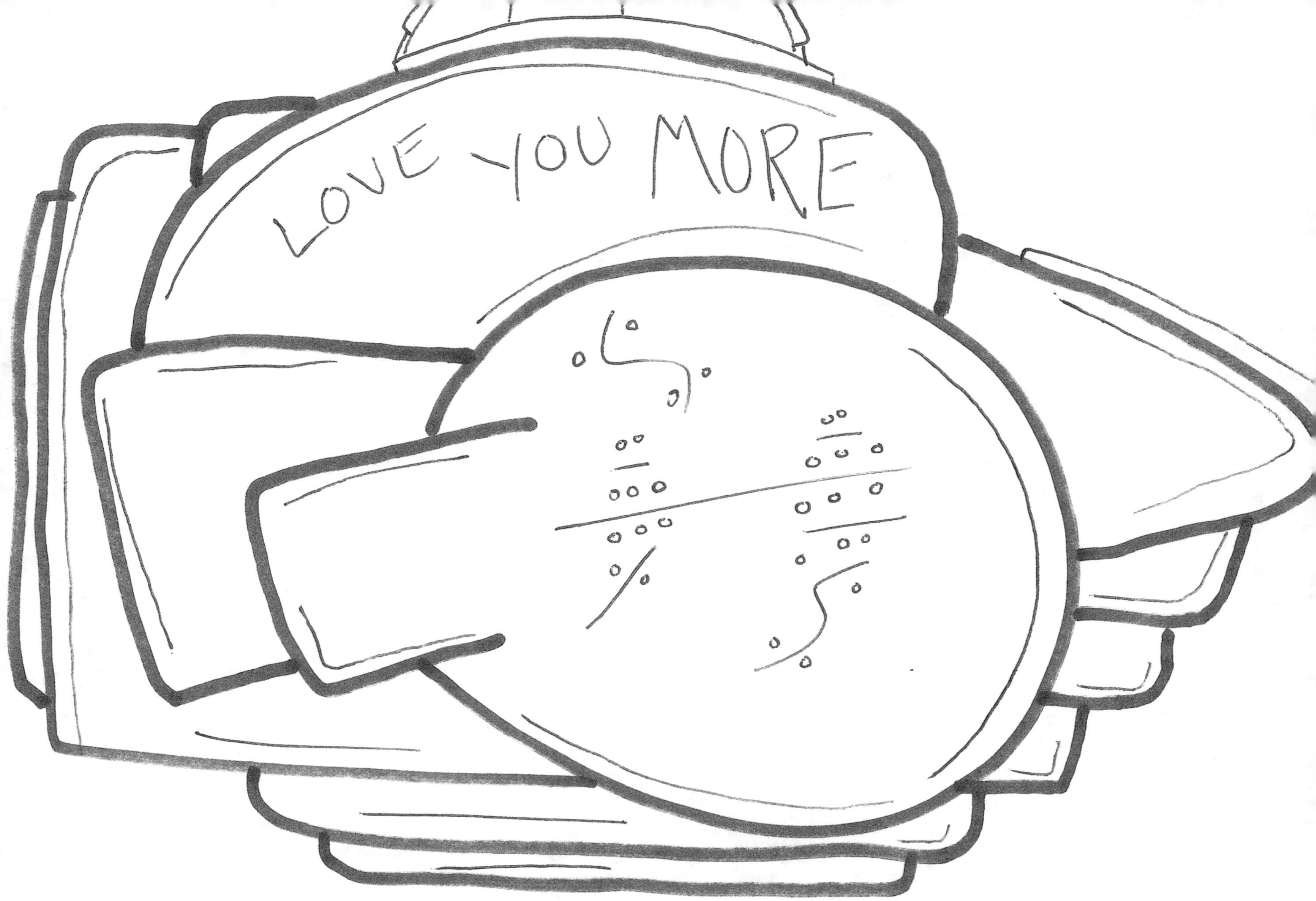
LOVE YOU MORE

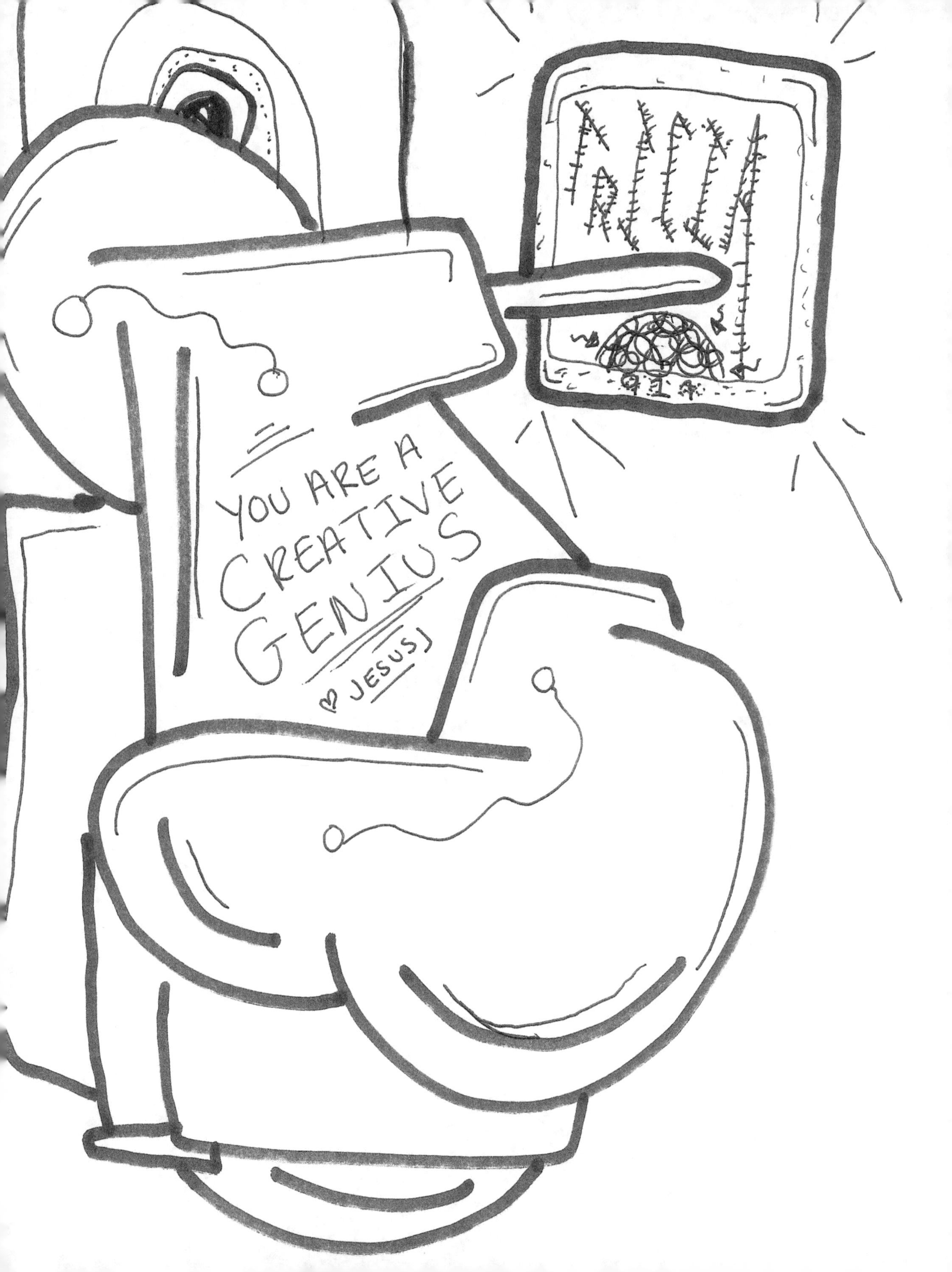
YOU ARE A
CREATIVE
GENIUS
♡ JESUS

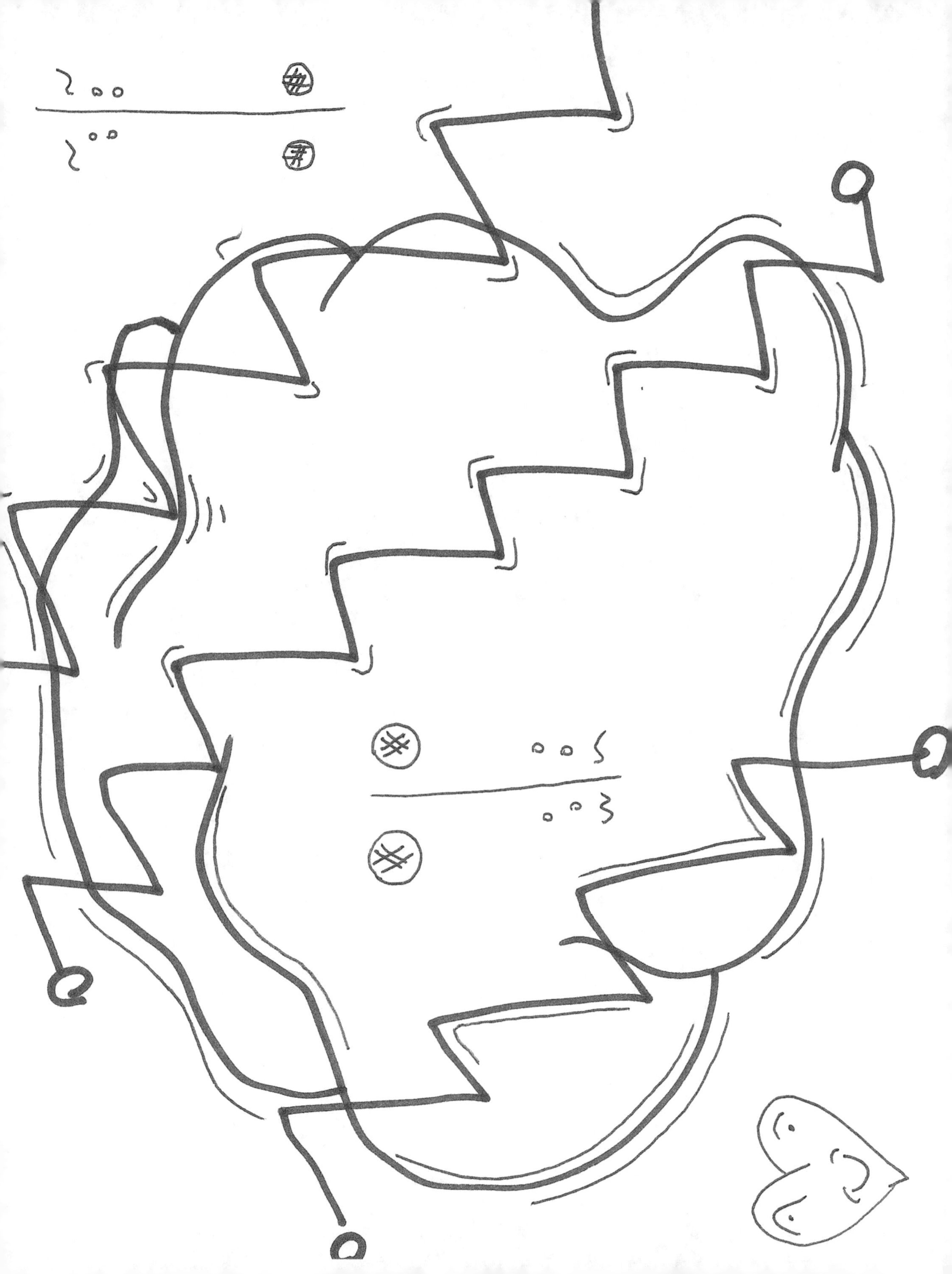

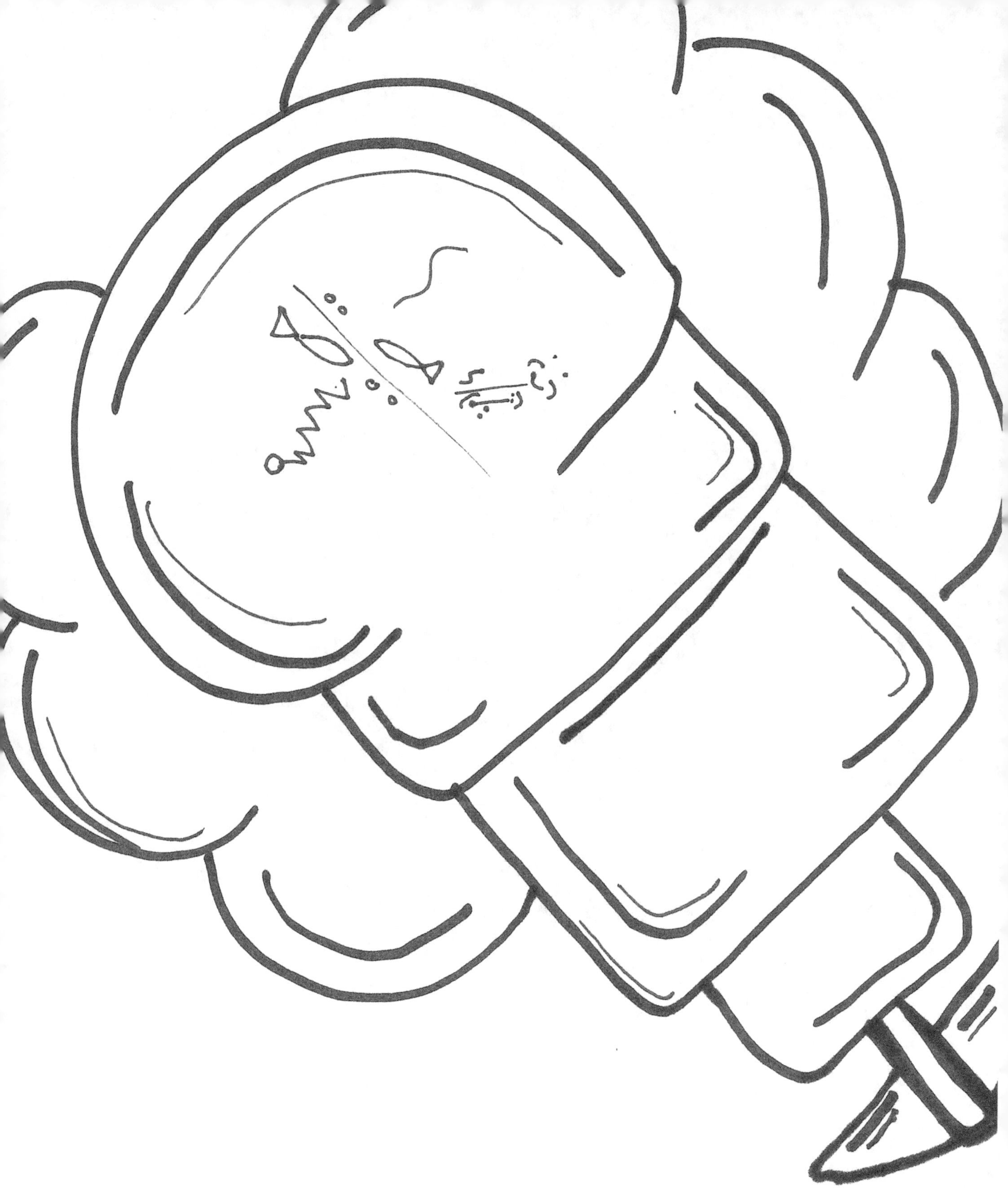

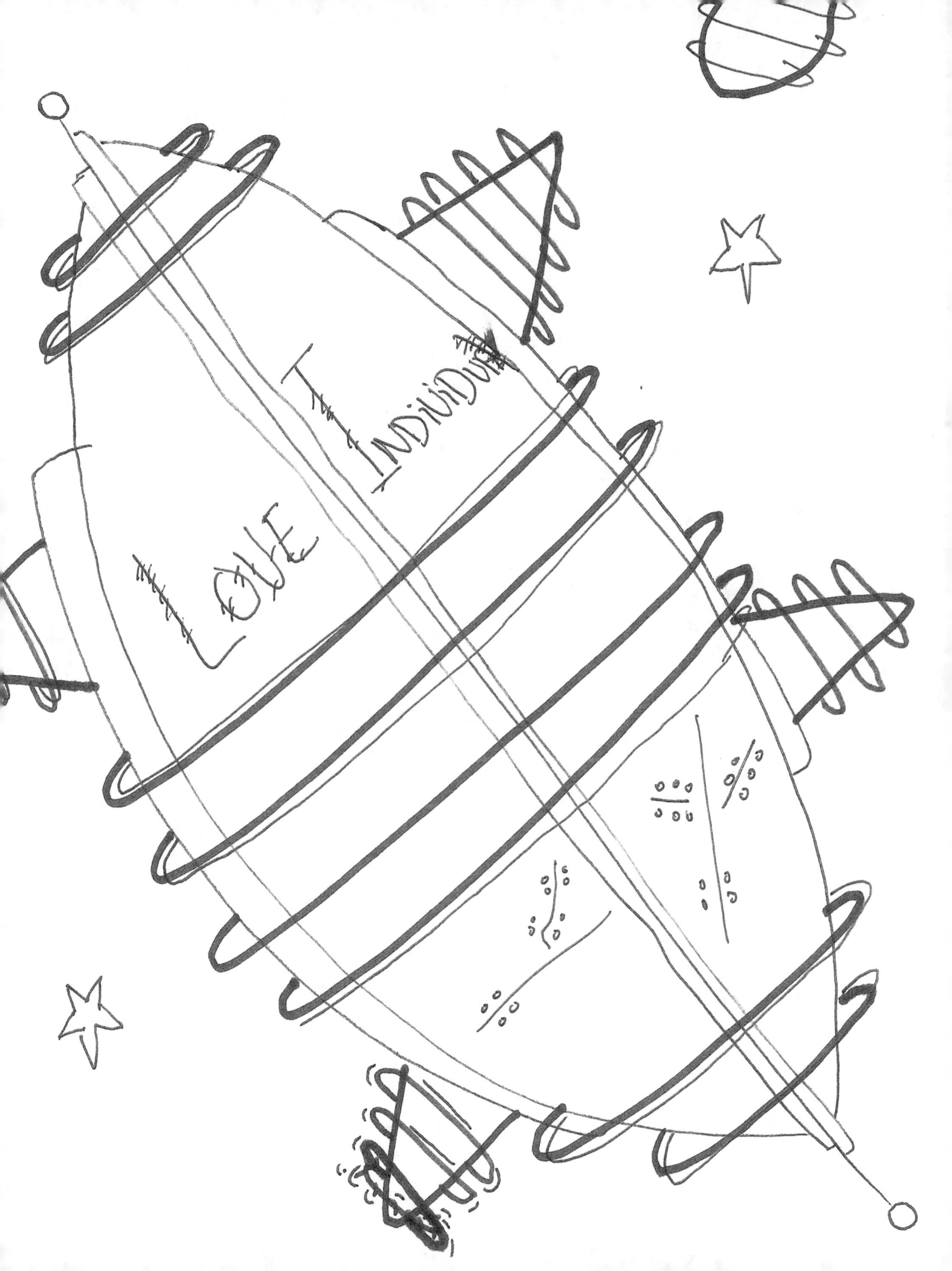
LOVE
INDIVIDU

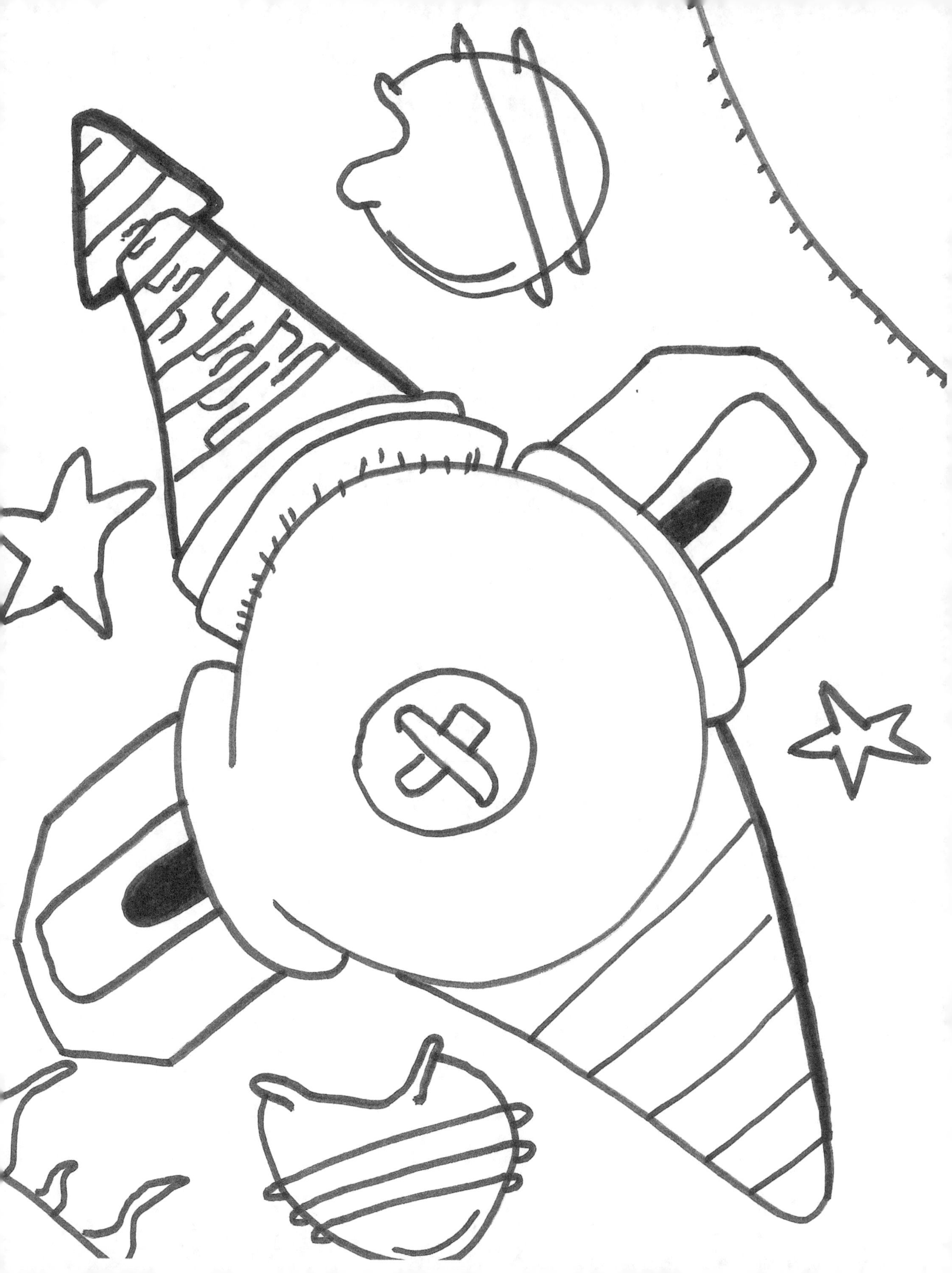

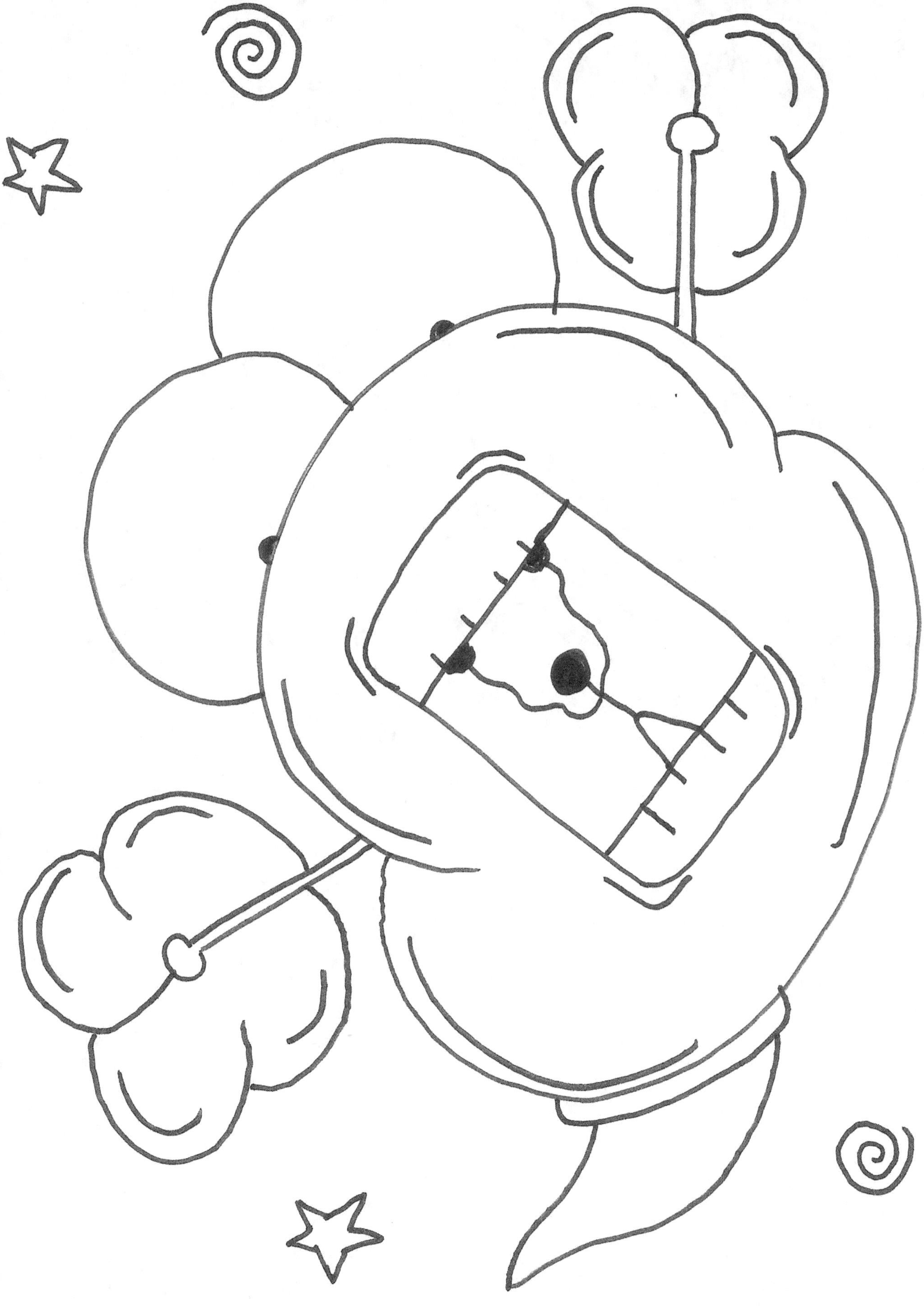

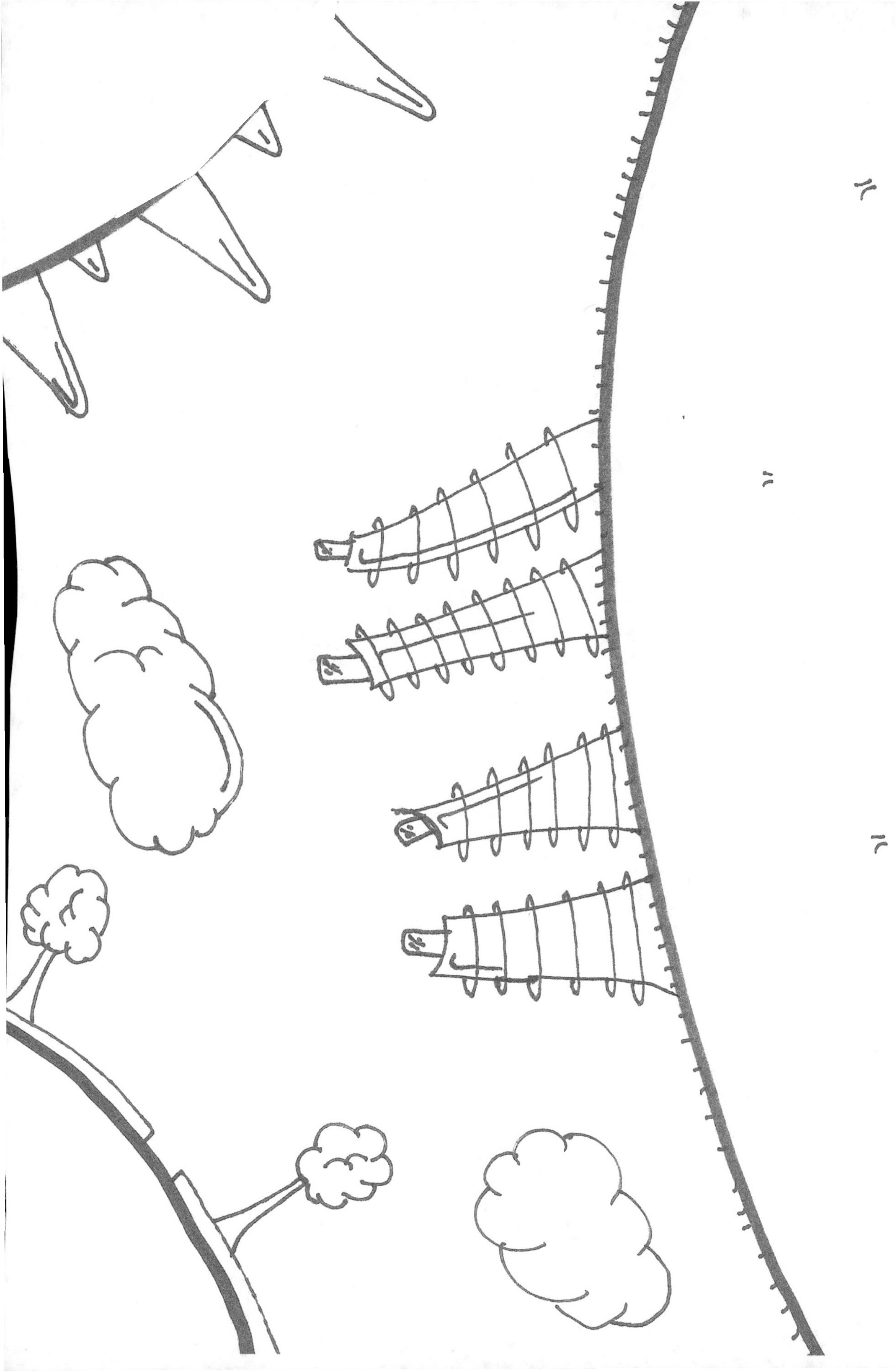

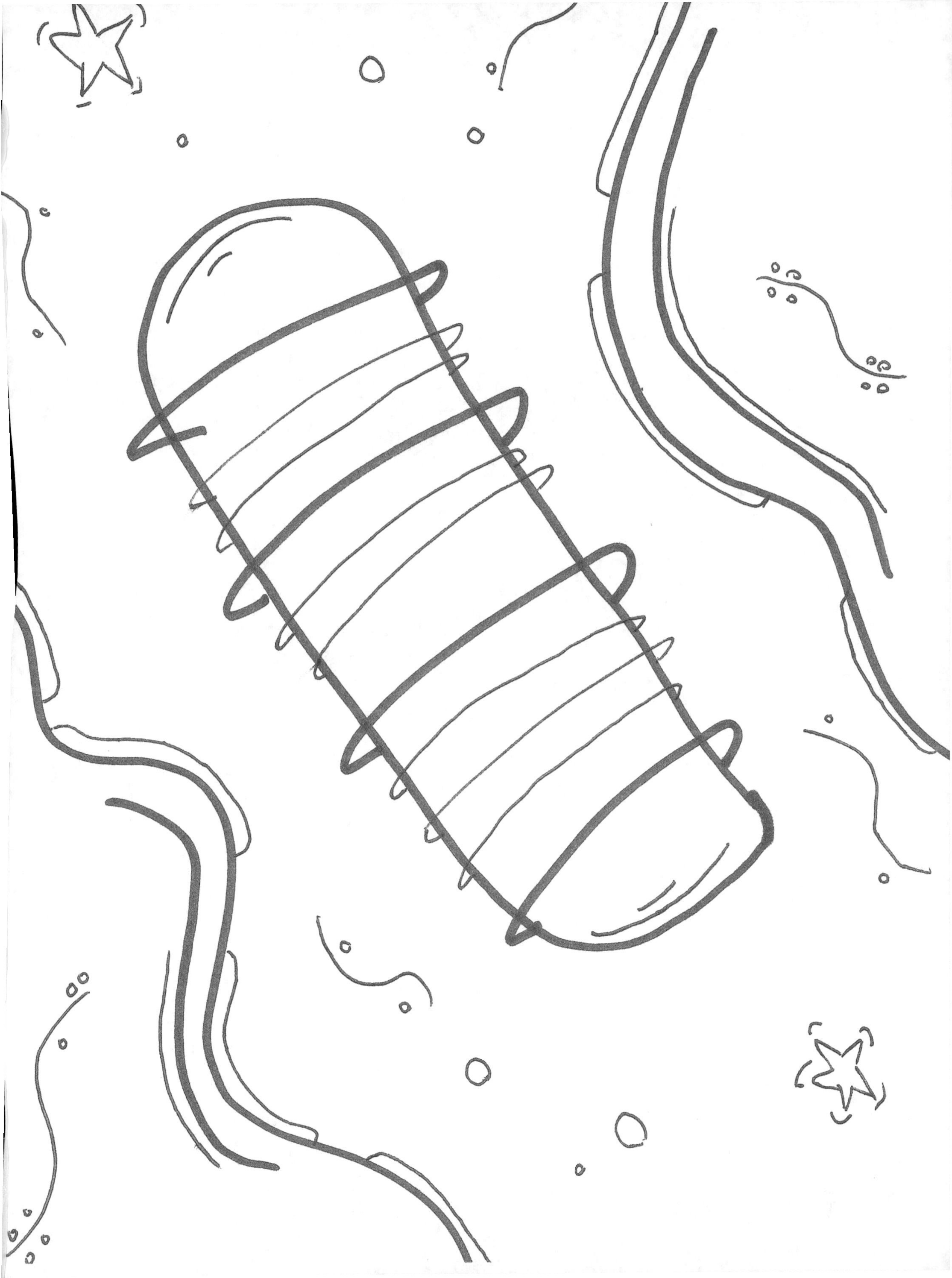

www.ingramcontent.com/pod-product-compliance
Lightning Source LLC
Chambersburg PA
CBHW081828170526
45167CB00007B/2749
9781494844141